P9-CDL-093

The Word Museum

The Most Remarkable English Ever Forgotten

Jeffrey Kacirk

A Touchstone Book
Published by Simon & Schuster
New York   London   Toronto   Sydney   Singapore

TOUCHSTONE
Rockefeller Center
1230 Avenue of the Americas
New York, NY 10020

Designed by Ruth Lee

Manufactured in the United States of America

9 10 8

Library of Congress Cataloging-in-Publication Data
Kacirk, Jeffrey.
The word museum : the most remarkable English ever forgotten
/ Jeffrey Kacirk.
p.   cm.
"A Touchstone book."
1. English language—Obsolete words. I. Title.
PE1667 .K38 2000
423'.1—dc21   00-030098

ISBN 0-684-85761-8

ACKNOWLEDGMENTS

This collection is dedicated to Lewis Carroll, who was inspired by antiquated English to imagine words for, among other things, his famous "Jabberwocky," which begins,

> 'Twas brillig, and the slithy toves
> Did gyre and gimble in the wabe:
> All mimsy were the borogroves,
> And the mome raths outgrabe.

Many thanks are due to my wife, Karen, for her daily moral support and her interest in old words. My agent, Bonnie Solow, has in a very real sense made this work possible with her special talent for locating the right publisher. In addition, I am grateful to Vincent P. O'Hara Jr., Bruce Newling, and Andy Swapp for their input in the selection process, along with Virginia MacRay for her editing expertise.

I would also like to acknowledge the British Library and the Bodleian Library for access to their unique collections of books and manuscripts.

> And one might therefore say of me that in this book I have only made up a bunch of other people's flowers, and that of my own I have only provided the string that ties them together.
>
> MICHEL DE MONTAIGNE (1533–92)

INTRODUCTION

The English language, as the largest and most dynamic collection of words and phrases ever assembled, continues to expand, absorbing hundreds of words annually into its official and unofficial rolls, but not without a simultaneous yet imperceptible sacrifice of terms along the way. Fortunately, before their quiet disappearance, many of these reflections of antiquity, the "remnants of history which casually escaped the shipwreck of time," to use a phrase of Francis Bacon, were recorded in a variety of published and unpublished writings, including dictionaries and glossaries.

I still remember my first browse through one of these nineteenth-century lexicons, in which I failed to find a noteworthy entry for some time. Coupled with my initial enchantment was a bit of discouragement brought on by the sheer volume of words that had changed surprisingly little over a century and a half. But a few years later, I found renewed inspiration in Joseph Shipley's

Dictionary of Early English, a work densely packed with intriguing vignettes of bygone eras. As I located more of this type of historical reference, I began to realize that, despite their undeniable dusty-dryness, these yellowed time capsules could provide intimate glimpses of the past, while charting the evolution of English. Sensing the story that these archaisms had to tell, I began to compile a notebook of my favorites, and eventually developed the goal of organizing these gems into a form that would allow others to conveniently sample a diverse cross section of the best lexicographers without undue tedium.

Of particular interest to me have been the myriad elusive details of earlier times that tend to go unnoticed. In my schooling, I found that teachers and historians, because of their socially prescribed curricular attention toward larger social concepts, often bypassed the smaller and more personal expressions of social custom and conduct, often leaving the novel as the best lens with which to view forgotten elements of everyday life. Take, for instance, the long-defunct activity called *upknocking,* the employment of the *knocker up,* who went house to house in the early morning hours of the nineteenth century to awaken his working-class clients before the advent of affordable alarm clocks. Until encountering this entry, I had never thought about how people of this time managed to awaken with any predictability.

In putting together this retrospective, I was reminded many times of Charles Mackay, who in the introduction to his 1874 glossary, *Lost Beauties of the English Language,* appealed to his readers, and especially to writers and poets, to consider resurrecting some of the more colorful but obscure words he had highlighted, by using them in place of their drab modern counterparts. Mackay's work is characteristic of a largely nineteenth-century movement to record fading provincial and archaic language, an activity that was perceived to be necessary in part because of the culturally homogenizing influence of the expanding railroad on formerly isolated communities. This surge of interest among both amateur and professional wordsmiths in the British Isles involved the gathering and publication of terms not for their practical application in vocabulary building but because they were recognized as being of historical interest in their own right.

I based my selection of entries for *The Word Museum* on a number of subjective considerations, an important one being the "Jabberwocky factor"—the eccentric phonic essence of certain headwords, such as *crulge, gubbertushed*, and *kiddliwink*. As a tandem goal of mine was to spotlight endearing, rough-hewn, and humorous aspects of Old World life, other formerly plausible terms, such as *idle-worms, blink-fencer*, and *pastorauling*, were also selected. Many of these linguistic fossils are remarkable for their longevity, while others delight us because they describe persistent anachronisms, such as *stang*, an ancient vigilante-style chastisement for marital infidelity, which managed to survive into the twentieth century. Specifically, my bias has been in favor of expressions that not only offer insights into the nature of our living language but simultaneously illustrate telltale beliefs and customs.

In singling out material for this project, I passed over nearly all commonly understood standard English words, along with place-names and the bulk of the vocabulary from the realm of the naturalist, including the names of plants, animals, minerals, and chemical compounds, except for such noteworthy exceptions as *goatmilker*. I discarded the names of nearly every type of hardware, despite their sometimes curious meanings, along with almost all foreignisms, which, it might be argued, are often not particularly English anyway. The reader will, however, find a sampling of scientific-sounding Greek- and Latin-based words, like *nympholepsy, pornocracy,* and *ambidexter,* which were once known figuratively as *inkhorn terms* because of their origins in the ink holders of pedantic writers.

When similar or identical entries were found in multiple sources, I presented the best written, most revealing, or oldest descriptions. When an entry was found in a source, such as Wright's *Dialect Dictionary,* that credited an older one, I generally credited the earlier source. At times I included more than one etymological explanation to add depth to definitions, to allow the reader to decide which might be correct, and to give a sense of how subjective etymology can be. It should be noted that, particularly with regional words, reader familiarity with some entries is inevitable, as my intention was to put forth the most interesting expressions, not necessarily those that have disappeared completely.

Peppered throughout this work is an odd group of once common adjectives, adverbs, and abstract nouns that, while similar to modern words, look and sound strange to us today, such as *ruly, anywhen,* and *thrunched.* Certainly these abandoned forms once rolled off the tongue and into the ear without the perceptual thud they might convey to the sensibilities of many modern readers and listeners. A few of these seemed worth shedding light on because they illustrate an informal rule of thumb: modern words and phrases often sound less awkward than their archaic forerunners, which is somewhat akin to the proverb "History is written by the victors."

I gently reconstructed a small minority of definitions solely for the sake of clarity, brevity, and overall readability, yet I made every attempt to retain the integrity and charm of the original passages. Where unavoidable, I took the liberty of modernizing our linguistic ancestors' creative spelling and distinctive punctuation, added bracketed words of explanation, and in a few instances combined noncontiguous sentences by one author into a single, comprehensive description. These changes were often necessary to ensure not only the reader's understanding of an entry but the entry's ability to fit the format.

Author citations, found after each quotation, refer the reader to the bibliography. The dates of publication found there should be viewed as merely a clue to when a given expression was in effect. Most words were used at the time of publication listed, but it should be kept in mind that an entry's usage may well have occurred somewhat or much earlier (as in the glossaries of Shakespeare) and some entries may have remained current well beyond this date, even into modern times.

As important as it may be to examine the early cataloguers of English, my focus has been on showcasing the terms themselves. Nonetheless, an understanding of the lives and individual contributions of certain lexicographers can greatly enhance our appreciation of the formation of modern English. For an in-depth examination of the minds behind the dictionaries, I recommend Jonathon Green's 1996 work, *Chasing the Sun,* for its well-researched character sketches of prominent dictionary makers and their craft.

Although we are inevitably left with a less than complete profile of many of these abandoned expressions, their remains can kindle in us a sense of wonder about the development of not only the English language but, by extension, many Western social traditions. I hope that these remarkable philological relics, by offering a peep through a fence knothole at vanished times and modes of expression, will provide the reader heartfelt connections with the mystery-laden past.

abbey-lubber A slothful loiterer in a religious house, under pretence of sanctity and austerity. Compounded of *abbey* and Danish *lubbed,* fat. [Fenning]

abcedarian A person or book that teaches the alphabet. [Sheridan] A word formed from the first four [or five] letters of the alphabet. [Whitney] SEE *hornbook*

abortive Fine vellum made from the skin of a cast [stillborn] calf or lamb. [Kersey]

abracadabrant Marvelous or stunning; from *abracadabra,* a magic word used as a spell in the United States. [Barrère]

accubitus Lying together in the same bed, but without any venereal commerce. [J. Coxe]

Adam's ale Water. [Smith] From the supposition that Adam had nothing but water to drink. In Scotland, water for a beverage is called *Adam's wine*. [Brewer]

admiral's watch A good night's sleep, especially at night; a favorable opportunity to rest. [Irwin]

adulterine A child born of an adultress. [Sheridan] Adulterine children are more odious than the illegitimate offspring of single persons. [E. Chambers]

adventurers upon return Those travellers who lent money before they went [abroad], upon the condition of receiving more on their return from a hazardous journey. This was probably their proper title. [Nares]

aflunters In a state of disorder. "Her hair was all *aflunters*." *Yorkshire* [J. Wright]

aforcing Stretching the amount of a dish to accomodate more people, usually by adding eggs, grain or cheese. [Shipley]

a-gatewards This is a very common and, I may add, very remarkable expression. To go *a-gatewards* with any one is to accompany him part of his way home. *Gate* is the public highway; *wards* denotes direction, as in *home-wards, to-wards,* &c. To go *a-gatewards* was therefore to conduct a guest towards the high-road, the last office of hospitality, necessary both for guidance and for protection, when the high-way lay across an undisclosed and almost trackless country, amidst woods and morasses. [J. Hunter]

agglutinants Those medicines which have the power of uniting parts together. [Sheridan] SEE *colleticks*

album nigrum The excrement of mice and rats, formerly used both externally and internally as a remedy but now, very properly, abandoned. [Hoblyn]

alectromantia Divination by a cock. Draw a circle, and write in succession round it the letters of the alphabet; on each side of it lay a grain of corn. Then put a cock in the centre of the circle, and watch the grains he eats. The letters will prognosticate the answer. [From] Greek *alector,* cock, *manteia,* divination. [Brewer] SEE *gyromancy*

alegar A hybrid word springing from the Saxon *ale,* and the French *aigre* [sour]. It is ale or beer which has passed through the acetous fermentation, and is used as a cheap substitute for vinegar, in imitation of which this word has been formed. [J. Hunter]

ale-score A debt at an ale-house. According to Wedgwood, *score* was originally a "notch, then from the custom of keeping count by cutting notches on a stick, account, reckoning, number, the specific number of twenty being the number of knotches it was convenient to make on a single stick. When that number was complete, the piece on which they were made was *cut off* [French, *taillée*] and called a *tally.*" [Jackson] SEE *milkscore*

ale-taster An officer appointed in every court-leet to look to the assize and goodness of bread, ale and beer. [Kersey] Whatever might be their use formerly, their places are now regarded only as fine-cures [financial punishment] for decayed citizens. [Johnson]

allecter To wamble as a queasie stomacke dothe. [Cotgrave]

allemang Mixed together; a Wiltshire saying, when two flocks of sheep are accidentally driven together. [Grose, *PG*]

all sorts A slang term designating the drippings of glasses in saloons, collected and sold at half-price to drinkers who are not overly particular. [Clapin]

almanac-man The Surveyor of the Court of Sewers, so called because he sends notices to the dwellers, near the Trent, of times when high tides may be expected. [Peacock]

almner An officer of a king or prince's house whose function is carefully to collect the fragments of meat and victuals and distribute them every day . . . [and] likewise to receive and faithfully distribute cast horses, robes, money and other things given in alms. He ought also to excite the king with often admonitions, especially on festival days, to be bountiful in giving alms, and to beseech that his rich robes may not be given to parasites, maskers and stage-players, or the like. [Blount, *LD*]

alms-drink The leavings of drink, or such as might be given away in alms; in other words, "heel-taps." [Phin] SEE *heel-taps*

alytarch He who seeth that good rule be kept at common games and exercises. [Blount, G, 1656]

amativeness A term in phrenology indicative of a propensity to the sexual passion. It is common to men [and] the lower animals. Its organ is the cerebellum, and its energy is denoted by the extent of the space on each side of the head between the mastoid process, immediately behind the ear and the spine of the occipital bone. From *amo*, to love. [Hoblyn] SEE *phrenology*

ambidexter It is intended by this Latin word to designate one who plays both sides. In a legal sense it is taken for a juror or embraceor who takes money from both parties for giving his verdict. This is seldom or never done in the United States. [Bouvier]

ambosexans Male and female. [Coles] SEE *transfeminate*

andrantomy The dissection of the human body, particularly that of the male. [Quincy]

angel-bread Purgative cakes made of spurge [a "corrosive herb"], oatmeal and ginger. [T. Wright]

answer-jobber One who makes a trade of writing answers. [Worcester]

anti-guggler A straw, or crooked tube, introduced into a spirit cask or neck of a bottle, to suck out the contents, commonly used in 1800 to rob the captain's steward's hanging safe in hot climates. [Smyth] SEE *tap the admiral, ullage*

antipodes People who live on the other side of the earth to us, going with their feet directly against ours. [Kersey]

anywhen At any time. This word is in common use among the common peasants in the south of England, but has not yet been admitted to the honors of the dictionary. . . . This word seems quite as well entitled to a literary position as *anyhow, anywhere, anywhither,* or *anywise,* all of which are recognised in English. [Mackay]

aphiocem A composition of flour and buds of hemp. [J. Coxe]

aproneer A shopkeeper; a tradesman. [Farmer]

aquabob An icicle; [from] Latin *aqua*, water. *Kent* [Holloway]

archilaugh The return which one, who has been treated in an inn or tavern, sometimes reckons himself bound in honour to make to the company. When he calls for his bottle, he is said to "give them his archilaugh." [Jamieson]

arfname An heir; from Old Norse *arfr*, inheritance, [and] *niman*, to take; used from the tenth to thirteenth centuries. [Shipley]

arithmetician Steevens explains it as one "that fights by the book of arithmetic." [Phin] SEE *iatromathematique*

armshot Arm's length. [Robinson, GMY] SEE *eyeshot*

astrotheology

aspirin-hound One addicted to extensive use of aspirin. Addicts either take it internally or roll the powdered tablet in cigarettes. [Goldin]

astrotheology Divinity founded on the observation of celestial bodies. [Browne] SEE *planet-ruler, stelliscript, weatherspy*

aubades Songs, or instrumentall music, sung, or playd under anyone's chamber window in the morning. [Phillips] SEE *hunt's-up*

audit ale Extra strong ale, supposed to be drunk when the accounts are audited. [Hotten]

avering When a begging boy strips himself and goes naked into a town with a fals[e] story of being cold and stript to move compassion and get better cloaths, this is call'd *avering*, and *to goe a-avering*. [Kennett] SEE *jarkman*

awblaster A cross-bowman. [Jamieson]

awhape To strike, to confound . . . The Teutonic language had anciently *wapen*, to strike, or some such word from which *weapons*, or offensive arms, took their denomination. [Johnson]

azzardly Poor, ill-thriven; [from] *azzard*, a wayward child. [Carr]

babies-in-the-eyes The miniature reflection of himself which a person sees in the pupil of another's eye on looking closely into it. Our old poets make it an employment of lovers to look for them in each other's eyes. [Halliwell] Sportively called by our ancestors a "little boy" or "baby," and made the subject of many amorous allusions. [Nares] SEE *love-tooth, sheep's-eye*

babyshed Deceived by childish tales. [T. Wright]

back-friend Pretended or false friend, with punning allusion to the sergeant approaching from behind or clapping the man on the back. [Onions]

backspang A trick or legal quirk by which one takes advantage of another, after the latter had supposed every thing in a bargain or settlement to be finally adjusted. [Jamieson]

backsters Wide, flat pieces of board, which are strapped on the feet, and used to walk over loose beach on the sea coast [in] Kent and East Sussex. Similar things are used in Hampshire for walking on the soft mud deposited in harbours by the sea, and they are called *mud-pattens*. [Holloway]

badge of poverty In the reign of William III, those who received parish relief had to wear a badge. It was the letter *P*, with the initial of the parish to which they belonged, in red or blue cloth, on the shoulder of the right sleeve. [Dyer]

baffound To stun and perplex. [Robinson, GMY]

bairman A poor insolvent debtor, left *bare naked*, who was obliged to swear in court that he was not worth more than five shillings and five pence. [Bailey] SEE *white bonnet*

bait-pot A large pot for cooking food for horses. [Warrack] SEE *nacks*

ballop The old name for the flap in the forepart of the breeches which is buttoned up; in English, formerly called the *codpiece*. [Jamieson]

banting *Doing banting*, reducing superfluous fat by living on meat diet and abstaining from farinaceous food and vegetables, according to the method adopted by William Banting [1796–1878], a London cabinet-maker, once a very fat man. The word was introduced about 1864. [Brewer] SEE *dry diet*

barber's music Rough music. A guitar or some such instrument was formerly kept in a barber's shop for the amusement of customers while waiting their turn. The instrument, being thrummed on by all comers, was not usually of much excellence. [Davies]

barguest A ghost, all in white, with large saucer eyes, commonly appearing near gates or stiles called *bars* [in] Yorkshire. [Grose, *PG*] An apparition said to take the form of a white cow, a horse, or a big black dog which, on dark nights leaps upon the shoulders of the scared wayfarer. [Taylor] The use of the barghast now is to alarm naughty children into order and obedience, though there may still be a few children of a larger growth who think that in the winter nights this spectre may be seen at the corners of streets or near half-broken walls, with his long teeth and saucer eyes. [J. Hunter] SEE *black cow*

barley-child A child born in wedlock but which makes its advent within six months of marriage. The metaphor lies in the allusion to the time which elapses between barley sowing and barley harvest. [Jackson] SEE *double-sib, queer-gotten, side-slip, special-bastard*

barlihood A fit of obstinancy or violent ill temper; also used to denote a state of drunkenness. [Grant]

barnacle-goose, tree-goose These are the birds that . . . were believed to be generated out of wood, or rather a species of shell . . . often found sticking to the bottoms of ships . . . and were called *tree-geese*. [Pennant] This bird, which was known in the British Isles only as a visitor, became the subject of a curious popular fable, not yet extinct, being believed to be bred from a tree growing on the sea-shore, either from the fruit of the tree or as itself the fruit, or from a shell-fish which grew on this tree. [Whitney]

barring-out A yearly custom amongst schoolboys of *barring* or excluding the schoolmaster from school on a particular day. [Addy]

bathing-machine A covered vehicle used at the seaside resorts of Britain in which bathers dressed. It is driven into the water to a sufficient distance to suit the bather. [Whitney]

batilbaby An office in forests. [T. Wright] SEE *tineman*

batterfanged

batterfanged Beaten and beclawed, as a termagant will fight with her fists and nails. [Robinson, GWW] [Hotten] SEE *clapperclaw*

beasts of venery The hart, hind, hare, boar and wolf. [Bailey]

beblubbered Swollen. [Worcester]

bedfellow It was formerly customary for men, even of the highest rank to sleep together, and the term bedfellow implies great intimacy. . . . Cromwell is said to have obtained much of his intelligence during the civil wars from common men with whom he slept. [Halliwell]

bedswerver An adulteress, one who *swerves* from the fidelity of the marriage bed. [Nares] SEE *preternuptual*, *wedbreaker*

bee-ale A species of beer, or rather mead, made from the refuse of honey. [Jamieson]

beestings The first milk after a cow has calved, which is thick and clotty, and in Northampton called *cherry-curds*. [Allied with] German *biest-milch*, Anglo-Saxon *beost*, French *callebouté*, curded or *beesty*, as the milk of a woman that is newly delivered . . . The earth was, in the Middle Ages, supposed to be surrounded by a sea of so thick a substance as to render navigation impossible. This was called *mer bétée* in French, and *lebermer* in German, the "loppered sea." [Wedgwood]

beever-time A quarter of an hour's relaxation allowed to the boys in the middle of the afternoon school in summer to give them an opportunity of disposing of *beevers*, a portion of bread and allowance of beer laid out in Winchester

School hall; from the Old French *boivre, beivre,* to drink. [Cope]

beggar's bed The bed which in farm and country houses was allowed to beggars; it was generally made up in the barn. [Mactaggart]

beggars' velvet Downey particles which accumulate under furniture from the negligence of housemaids. [Hotten] SEE *culf*

begrumpled Displeased. *Somersetshire* [T. Wright]

begrutten Showing the effects of much weeping. [Whitney] SEE *gowl*

behounc'd Tricked up and made fine; a metaphor taken from a horse's *hounces* [collar ornaments], which is part of the furniture of a cart-horse which lies spread upon his collar. [Ray]

bellibone A woman excelling both in beauty and goodness. [Johnson] From French *belle,* beautiful, and *bonne,* good. [Stormonth] SEE *cowfyne, pigsnye, snoutfair*

bellitude Beauty of person; loveliness; elegance; neatness. [Cockeram]

belly-pinched Starved; hungry. [Phin]

belly-rack The art of gormandising; [from] *racking,* or stretching the belly. [Jamieson]

belly-vengeance Weak, sour beer, of which he that gets the most, gets the worst share. [Carr]

bend-leather A boy's phrase for a slide on a pond when the ice is thin and bends. [Addy]

besom-clean Clean as a broom can make a floor without its having been washed. [T. Hunter]

bibitory A muscle that draws the eye down towards the cup when one drinks. [Bailey] SEE *swine-greun*

biblioklept A book-thief; one who purloins or steals books. [Whitney]

bibliothecary Keeper of a library. [Coles]

biggening Uprising of women. [Coles] SEE *crying-cheese*

bilf, bulf Something large and clumsy . . . A stout, podgy person was called a *bulfie*. [Grant]

Billy-winks A child's term for "sleepy." Said of a sleepy child: "*Billy-winks* is comin'." [Taylor] SEE *wink-a-peeps*

bird-duffer A dishonest dealer in birds who "makes up" his wares, either by painting the plumage of live birds, or by fabricating bird-skins, affixing false labels, etc. [Whitney]

bird-organ A small barrel-organ used in teaching birds to sing. [Ogilvie]

bishopped Milk or pottage burned in the process of heating. [Holloway] *The bishop has set his foot in it*, a saying in the North used for milk that is burnt in boiling. Formerly, in days of superstition, whenever a bishop passed through a town or village, all the inhabitants ran out in order to receive his blessing. This frequently caused the milk on the fire to be left till burnt to the vessel, and gave origin to the above allusion. [Grose, *PG*]

black-act A law which makes it felony to appear armed with

bird-duffer

the face blackened, for the purpose of taking game. [Stormonth]

black cow An imaginary black cow said to tread on one when calamity comes. [Grant] "The black ox has not trod upon his foot," [said] of one that has not been pinch'd with want. [B.E.] SEE *barguest*

black rent Extractions formerly levied by native chieftains in

Ireland, particularly upon districts where English were settled. [Whitney]

bleezed Signifies the state of one on whom intoxicating liquor begins to operate. It especially denotes the change produced in the expression of the countenance. [Jamieson] SEE *cheeping-merry*

blepharon He that hath great eyebrows. [Coles] SEE *man-browed*

blindman's dinner A dinner unpaid for. A dinner in which the landlord is made the victim. [Brewer]

blind tam A bundle of rags, carried by female mendicants, made up so as to pass for a child, in order to excite compassion and secure charity. [Jamieson]

blinked-beer Bad beer. Probably from . . . *to blink the question*, to evade. A question that is *blinked* is lost sight of, so beer that is spoiled is lost. *Norfolk, Suffolk* [Holloway]

blink-fencer A person who sells spectacles, especially on the street. [Hotten]

bloodguiltless Free from the guilt of shedding blood, or murder. [Lyons]

bloody-hand One of the four kinds of offences in the king's forest, by which the offender is supposed to have killed a deer. In Scotland, in such like crimes they say, "Taken in the fact, or with the *red hand*." [Blount, *LD*] SEE *dog-draw*, *yburpananseca*

bloss A term of endearment; a buxom young woman; [from]

blossom. Scotland, Northern England [J. Wright] SEE *cowfyne*, *pigsnye, snoutfair*

bloten Fond, as children are of their nurses. [Ray] Perhaps derived from Anglo-Saxon *bloten*, to sacrifice, to worship. [Leigh]

blowze, blowsabella Rough, red-faced wench. As a substantive, this word is now very rare, but *blouzy*, rough, romping, hoidenish, is not an uncommon word applied to females. [Elworthy] A woman whose hair is dishevelled and hanging about her face; a slattern. [Grose, *DVT*]

blutterbunged Confounded, overcome by surprise. *Lincolnshire* [J. Wright] SEE *gloppened*

boiling-piece A piece of tough meat only suitable for boiling. Applied to anything tough or difficult to manage. A termagant wife is said to be a boiling-piece. [Taylor]

bomullock To make one change one's mirth into sorrow; a threatening used by parents or nurses when their children are troublesome or unseasonably gay, especially when they cannot be lulled to sleep. It is said to be a composite of two Celtic words. *Bw* is terror, or which causes it. The children in France . . . cry *bou* when they wish to affright their comrades. Gaelic *mullach*, primarily an eyebrow, is used to denote knotted or gloomy brows. Hence, *bomullach* is equivalent to the grisly ghost, the spectre with the dark eye-brows. [Jamieson]

bonksman A man who works at the mouth of a coal-pit. [Taylor]

book-scorpion A species of arachnidan, the *Chelifer cancroides*, often found in old books. [Ogilvie]

borrower's cap The borrower is supposed to be ever ready to off with his cap, and show compliance to him from whom he wishes to obtain a loan. [Phin] SEE *hat-worship*, *off-capped*

bottle-chart Those on which the set of surface currents are exhibited, derived from papers [bearing date, latitude and longitude] found on bottles which have been thrown overboard for that purpose, and washed up on the beach, or picked up by other ships. [Smyth] The time between the throwing of such bottles and their recovery on shore has varied from a few days to sixteen years, and the distance from a few miles to five thousand miles. [Whitney]

bottomry A contract for borrowing money on the keel or *bottom* of a ship, so that the commander binds the ship herself that if the money be not paid at the time appointed, the creditors shall have the ship. [Falconer]

bouffage A satisfying meal; [from] Old French *bouffer*, to swell. [Skeat] Any meat that, eaten greedily, fils the mouth, and makes the cheeks to swell; cheeke-puffing meat. [Cotgrave]

bouillands In cookery, little pies made of breasts of capons minced with udders. [Bailey]

bowdlerize To emasculate through squeamishness. [Hotten] To expurge a book in editing it. Thomas Bowdler, in 1818, gave to the world an expurgated edition of Shakespeare's works. We have also *bowdlerite*, *bowdlerist*, *bowdlerizes*, *bowdlerism*, *bowdlerisation*, etc. [Brewer]

bowelhive An inflammation of the bowels, to which children are subject. According to some, it is owing to what medical men call *intersusceptio*, or one part of the intestines being inverted. [Jamieson] SEE *illiack passion*

bowssen The Cornish call this immersion *boossenning*, from *beuzi* or *bidhyzi* . . . signifying "to dip or drown." . . . A very singular manner of curing madness in the parish of Altarnun was to place the disordered in mind on the brink of a square pool. The patient, having no intimation of what was intended was, by a sudden blow on the breast, tumbled into the pool, where he was tossed up and down by some persons of superior strength till, being quite debilitated, his fury forsook him. He was then carried to church, and certain masses sung over him. [Borlase] If there appeared small amendment, he was bowssened again and again. [Carew]

brade *To brade of a man* is to be, or act, like him; perhaps from Anglo-Saxon *bred*, fraud or cunning, as much as to say he makes use of the same arts and methods. [Watson]

brandy-cleek The palsey in the leg in consequence of hard drinking. [Jamieson]

brawn-fallen Thin; having the brawny or muscular part of the body fallen away; shrunk in the muscles. [Nares]

bread-rasp A rasp used by bakers in removing the burned crust of loaves and rolls, especially of French rolls. [R. Hunter] SEE *kissingcrust, tinker's toast*

breem A term applied to the female swine when she desires the male. Our ancestors had a variety of terms appropriated to different animals for expressing the desire of the male, some of which still remain. As breem distinguishes the sow, the female cat is said to *cate*, the cow to *eassin*, &c. [Jamieson] SEE *clicketing, eassin, towrus*

brewing-main A drinking-bout of new ale after a home-brewing. [Taylor]

bricklayer's clerk A contemptuous expression for lubberly pretenders to having seen "better days," but who were forced to betake themselves to sea-life. [Smyth]

bridlegged The Cheshire farmer, who holds that the perfect form of female beauty consists more in strength than in elegance of limbs, often uses this contemptuous appellation to any female whose limbs happen to be somewhat slenderer than he has in his own mind fixed on as a criterion of symmetry and taste. [From] the Anglo-Saxon root *brid*, the young of any bird. [Leigh]

brizzle To scorch near to burning . . . to burn slightly or singe. [Robinson, GMY]

broddler A toothed instrument for making holes of an irregular shape. A woman who kept school at Eckington used to prick or *brod* the children in the forehead with a sharp instrument which she called a *broddler*. She said she was driving sense into them. [Addy]

broken music Some instruments, such as viols, violins, flutes, etc., were formerly made in sets of four, which when played together formed a "consort." If one or more of the instruments of one set were substituted for the corresponding

broken music

ones of another set, the result was no longer a consort, but *broken music*. [Phin]

brought home A bicycle is "taken abroad" when taken to pieces, and "brought home" when it is put together. A door is "brought home" when closed. [Peter]

browis Pieces of bread soaked in water and afterwards saturated with fat. [From] Welsh *brywis*. [Carr] SEE *fatty-cakes, sowl*

brownstudy Gloomy meditation. [Browne] Absence of mind; apparent thought, but real vacuity. The corresponding French expression explains it—*sombre réverie. Sombre* and *brun* both mean sad, melancholy, gloomy, dull. [Brewer] Very common, even in educated society, but hardly admissible in writing . . . It is derived . . . from "brow study" [and] the Old German *braun*, or *aug-braun*, an eye-brow. [Hotten]

bruffed Thickly clothed. [Mactaggart]

bruzzle To make a great a-do, or stir. [Thoresby]

bubulcitate To cry like a cow boy. [Cockeram] To do the office of a *bubulcus*, or cowheard. [Phillips]

buckswanging A punishment used by grinders and other workmen for idleness, drunkenness, &c. The offender is jostled against a thorn hedge or a wall. It requires four men to do this, two to hold the offender's arms and two to hold his legs. Grinders generally *buckswang* a man against the wall of the grinding wheel. [Addy]

bull-jumpings Milk drawn from the cow after the calf has sucked. Called also *stroakings*. [Grose, SPG]

bull's-noon Midnight; a bull frequently breaking forth at that hour in search of adventures, as though it were mid-day instead of mid-night. *Suffolk, Norfolk* [Holloway]

bull-speaking Boasting language. [Nares]

bumwhush Ruin, obscurity, annihilation. [J. Wright] When anything has made a noise for some time, and it is then quashed, it is said to have "gone to the *bumwhush*." This is too often the way with people of great popularity; they have their day, and then go to the bumwhush. [Mactaggart]

bunting time When the grass is high enough to hide young men and maids. [B.E.]

burdalone The last child surviving in a family; the "lonely bird." [Mackay] SEE *nestcock*

burl To pour out ale to labourers. [Carr] A *burler* is a man whose duty it is to attend at suppers and similar occasions to . . . see that no glass is empty. I know a man near Leeds who rejoices in the title of a "professional burler." [Wilkinson]

burying-drink Warm ale, spiced and sweetened, served to the guests at a funeral in quart mugs with lemon peel twisted round the handle thereof. *Lancashire* [J. Wright]

butterine A substance or composition of clarified fat and butter, or fat alone, spiced and flavored. [Stormonth] An artificial butter made from animal fat churned with milk and water, or from milk churned with some sweet butter and the yolks of eggs. [Annandale] SEE *cruddy-butter*

butts and bounds Words used in describing the boundaries of land. Properly speaking, *butts* are the lines at the ends, and *bounds* are those on the sides, if the land is rectangular shape. But in irregular shaped land, *butts* are the points or corners where the boundary lines change direction. [Tayler]

buzznack An old organ, out of order and playing badly. *Yorkshire* [J. Wright]

by planets Irregularly; capriciously, in the same sense as a crazy person is said to be *moonstruck*. The rain falls *in planets*, means it falls partially. [Holloway] SEE *falling-weather*

cabobble To mystify, puzzle, confuse. *East Anglia, Cornwall* [J. Wright]

caddis Surgeon's lint for dressing wounds. [Ogilvie]

cade-lamb A pet lamb; one weaned and brought up in the house. [Crabb] Blount derives it from the Latin *casa* [house]; Skinner from an old French word, *cadeler,* to breed tenderly. [Carr] A *cade-child* is a child that has been brought up with excessive care and tenderness. [J. Hunter]

cag-mag Unwholesome or inferior meat. [Allied with] *cag-butcher,* a man who buys animals that have died a natural death, and also unsound animals; to slaughter, with the view of selling their flesh as "butcher's-meat." [Jackson] The word, in the language of Scotland, signifies an old goose. . . . The superannuated [old] geese and ganders which, by a long

cag-mag

course of plucking, prove uncommonly tough and dry. [Pennant] SEE *hylden, wangary*

calenture A burning fever, a distemper peculiar to sailors, wherein they imagine the sea to be green fields, and will throw themselves into it if not restrained. [Bailey] SEE *hydromania*

camelopardal This beast is engendered of a camel and a female libbard [leopard]. The head of the camelopardal is like a camel's, his neck like a horse's, and his body like a hart's. The color of this beast is for the most part red and white mixed together, therefore very beautiful. . . . His neck is diversely colored and is fifteen feet long. . . . They are very tractable and easy to be handled, so that a child may lead them with a small cord about their head and, when any come to see them, they willingly . . . turn themselves round . . . to show their soft hairs and beautiful color, being, as it were, proud to ravish the eyes of the beholders. [Topsell]

camel-swallower Applied to a weakly credulous person, or to one who is punctilious in small matters while negligent of greater. [Worcester] SEE *penny-wisdom*

carfumish To diffuse a very bad smell. The latter part of the word seems to be allied to French *fumeuse*, smoky, and Old English *fewmishing*, the ordure of a deer. [Jamieson] SEE *feff, odor of sanctity, natkin*

cark To be fretfully anxious. [Mackay]

carpet-knight A denomination given to men of peaceable professions, who are raised to the dignity of knighthood. They take the appellation *carpet* because they usually receive their honours from the king's hands in the court, kneeling on a carpet. By this they are distinguished from knights created in the camp or field of battle on account of their military prowess. [Barclay] One that ever loves to be in women's chambers. [Cotgrave] SEE *carpet-trade*

carpet-trade The behavior of a *carpet-knight*; flattery. [R. Hunter] SEE *carpet-knight*

carroon A rent for the privilege of driving a car or cart in the city of London. [Bailey]

carry-castle A name used by Elizabethan writers for an elephant. [Nares]

cataglottism A thrusting out of the tongue in kissing. [Phillips] See *deosculation, rabbit's-kiss*

catchpole An instrument consisting of a six-foot pole, furnished at the end with metal bars and springs so arranged as to catch and hold by the neck or a limb a person running away. [R. Hunter] One that catches by the poll, though now taken as a word of contempt. Yet in ancient times it was used without reproach for such as we call *Serjeants of the Mace*, bailiffs, or any other that we use to arrest men upon any action. [Blount, *LD*]

catholicum A remedy believed to be capable of curing all diseases—a panacea. [Dunglison] A general or common medicine that expels or corrects all ill humours, which is kept in shops. [Blancard]

cat-Latin Incoherent or idle talk; bad writing. [Kirkby] SEE *cronk, dog-Latin, thieves' Latin*

catrick A supposed disease of the roots of the fingers from too frequent handling of cats; a cataract supposed to effect the eyes of the first person that meets a cat which has lept over a dead body. [Warrack]

caul The membrane encompassing the head of some infants when born, and from early antiquity esteemed an omen of good fortune and a preservative against drowning. It was sought by the Roman lawyers with as much avidity as by modern voyagers. [Smyth] This caul . . . is frequently advertised for sale in our public papers and purchased by seamen. Midwives used to sell this membrane to advocates [attorneys] as an especial means of making them eloquent. [Brand]

causey-webs *To make causey-webs*, to neglect one's work, and idle in the streets. [Warrack] SEE *idle-worms*

celibataire Bachelor. [Davies]

cephaleonomancy Divination by a broiled asse's head. [Coles]

chafe litter *Chafe litter* is he that wyll plucke up the fether-bed or matrice, and pysse in the bedstraw, and wyl never ryse uncalled. This knave berayeth many tymes in the corners of his maister's chamber, or other places inconvenient, and maketh cleane hys shooes with the coverlet or curtaines. [Awdeley]

chalybeat Beer . . . wherein steel hath been quenched. [Coles]

chamber-lye Fermented urine, formerly used for laundry purposes, being a strong detergent. [Taylor] Formerly much used . . . as a drink for horses, to make them look well in their skins; also for outward application to harden horses' feet. [Brogden] SEE *lant*

chantepleur He that sings and weeps both together. [Coles] SEE *merry-go-sorry*

chaser A ram that has only one testicle. [Jamieson] SEE *wicker*

chatter-broth Tea. [Holloway] SEE *ninny-broth, purl, saloop*

cheeping-merry Half-drunk; "elevated." [J. Wright] SEE *bleezed*

chicken-pecked Under the rule of a child, as *hen-pecked* [is] under the rule of a woman. [Davies] SEE *woman-tired*

childwit Power to take a fine of your bondwoman [servant] gotten with child without your consent. [Coles] Within the manor of Writtle in Essex, every reputed father of a bastard gotten there, pays to the Lord for a fine [of] three shillings four pence, and the custom is there also called *childwit*. [Cowell] SEE *lotherwit*

chilihedron A figure of one thousand equal sides. [Webster] SEE *enneagon, umstroke*

chimble To crumble into very small fragments; to gnaw like a mouse or rat. [Mackay] SEE *motch, tooth-music*

chinees A familiar term for boiled peas, as sold in the streets. [Taylor] SEE *codders, peascod wooing, podware*

chirogymnast A mechanical apparatus for the exercising of a pianist's fingers; from Greek *cheir*, the hand, and *gymnastes*, a gymnast. [Zell]

chocolate-house A house where company is entertained with chocolate. [Johnson]

choosehow It means "under any circumstances," and is usually placed last in a sentence, but not always. "He will have to do it *choosehow*," he will have to do it under any circumstances. [Easther]

chowbent grubs Nails embedded in old timber, which spoil a carpenter's tools. *Cheshire* [J. Wright]

chrisom A child dying before baptism, or within a month of wearing the *chrisme* [christening] *cloath*. [Cocker] Still used in the local dialect, and probably signifies a pitiable object, such as a man reduced to a skeleton. [Easther] In some parts of England a calf kill'd before it is a month old is called a *chrisom-calf*. [Blount, G]

chummage A cruel custom in most of our gaols is that of the prisoners demanding of a newcomer garnish, footing, or as it is called in some of the London gaols, *chummage*. [Howard] SEE *foot-ale*

churching Thanksgiving after child-birth. It was the ancient custom for the female returning thanksgiving to be dressed in a white napkin. [Carr] Perils to soul and body accumulate about the great moments of birth, marriage and death. A woman after childbirth is the most dangerous thing on earth; demons are round about her, and if she goes to a river to wash, the fish will all go away. . . . Until she is *churched* after the child's birth, and, in the infant's case, until it is baptized, both are specially open to fairy influences. [Hull]

chyrme As applied to birds, it denotes the mournful sound emitted by them, especially when collected together before a storm. [Jamieson] SEE *renterfuge*

circumjovialists Certain stars that attend the planet Jupiter, called *Jupiter's satellites*. [Bailey]

clamberskull Strong drink that *clambers* up to the skull; a heady liquor. [Mackay]

clank-knapper A silver-tankard stealer. [Smith] SEE *peg-tankard*

clap-benny Infants, in the nurse's arms, are frequently requested to *clap-benny*, to clap their little hands, the only

clamberskull

means they have of expressing their prayers. [From] Icelandic *klapper*, to clap, and *bœne*, prayers. [Carr] Little
children are taught to *clap bene*, the latter word being pro-
nounced as a dissyllable. The action is the clapping of
hands, and the morality of the action is prayer; it is a mute
imploring of a blessing. [J. Hunter]

clapperclaw To tongue-beat; to scold. [Johnson] To scratch,
maul, fight in an unskillful manner; generally used of
women . . . Hence, *clapperclaw*, a noisy woman. [J. Wright]
SEE *batterfanged, curtain-lecture, xantippe*

clarke to the teethward [One] . . . such as maketh shew of
learning and be not learned. [Hollyband]

clawscrunt An old tree against which cattle rub themselves. [Mactaggart]

clicketing A fox is said to go *a-clicketing* when he is desirous of copulation. [Bailey] SEE *breem, eassin, towrus*

clicking-fork't Of a sheep, having two triangular-shaped pieces cut out of the ear, one on each side of the point; [allied with] *click't*, ear-marked in a particular way. [Dickinson] SEE *rounstow, shepherd's book*

climacterian One who is fond of a climax. [Davies]

clock-falling There is a superstition called *clock-falling* which is that, if a woman enter[s] a house after child-bearing and before being churched, the house-clock will immediately fall on its face. But a woman would never think of doing so, under any circumstances. [Robinson, *DOL*] SEE *churching*

clointer To make a noise with the feet. A person treading heavily with shoes shod with iron is said to clointer. [Brockett]

clowclash A state of confusion. [Robinson, GMY]

clumpst Hands stiff with cold are said to be *clumpst;* whence *clumsy.* [J. Hunter] Unhandy or made clumsy, as the hands are made by excess cold. [Watson]

clunter An unable stumbler. [Thoresby]

cockerate To brag. [Easther]

cock-throppled Having the "Adam's apple" largely developed. [Kirkby] From *thropple*, the wind-pipe. *Yorkshire* [Bailey]

cockwalk A fine or blackmail levied on a man who courts a woman residing out of the limits of his own parish. If this be a survival of an ancient practice or custom, it would appear that neither exogamy [marriage with non-locals] nor "marriage by capture" were usual at a remote period in this district; but that, on the contrary, the villagers . . . did not, in general, marry outside the limits of their own kindred by blood. [Addy]

codders Persons, chiefly Welch women, employed by the gardeners about London to gather peas. [Grose, PG] SEE *chinees, peascod wooing*

cold-fire Fuel laid for a fire, but unlighted. [Jackson]

colleticks Medicines that conglutinate, or glue together, as it were. [Bailey] SEE *agglutinants, scleroticks*

colonial goose A boned leg of mutton stuffed with sage and onions. In the early days, the sheep was almost the sole animal food. Mutton was then cooked in various ways to imitate other dishes. [Morris] SEE *pope's-eye*

colt-ale Ale given, or money paid for ale, by a person entering on a new employment to those already in it. Sometimes called *footing* or *foot-ale*. [Jennings] Ale claimed as a perquisite by the blacksmith on shoeing a horse for the first time. *To shoe the colt* is also a quaint expression of demanding a contribution from a person on his first introduction to any office or employment. [Carr] SEE *foot-ale*

colt's-tooth A love of youthful pleasure; a disposition to the practices of youth. [Johnson] Chaucer uses the word "coltish" for skittish. Horses have at three years old the colt's-tooth. The allusion is to the *colt's-teeth* of animals, a period of their life when their passions are strongest. [Brewer] Elderly persons of juvenile tastes are said to *have a colt's tooth*, a desire to shed their teeth once more, to see life over again. [Hotten] SEE *rudderish, sheep's-eye*

comassing It does not refer to begging by professional beggars, but it is the begging of a person on special occasions, fairs, &c., from his neighbour. It implies that the person who *goes comassing* is well known to all those he begs of. [Peacock] SEE *jarkman*

comediographer A writer of comedies. [Bailey]

comet-wine A term of praise to signify wine of superior quality. A notion prevails that the grapes in comet years are better in flavour than in other years, either because the weather is warmer and ripens them better, or because the comets themselves exercise some chemical influence on them. Thus, wine of the years 1811, 1826, 1839, 1845, 1852, 1858, 1861, &c., have a repute. [Brewer]

conskite To befoul with ordure, as when one's bowels are loosed with fear. [Shipley]

coppernose A name which is supposed to show a partiality on its owner's part for strong drink. Synonymous with *jolly nose. Grog-blossoms* are the jewels often set in a jolly nose. [Hotten]

cornage Horn-service. A kind of tenure in grand serjeantry. The service required was to blow a horn [*cornu*] when any invasion of the Scots was perceived. *Cornagium* was money paid instead of the old service. *Northern England* [Brewer]

corpse-gate In one or two of the churches about here there are still these old structures where the bearers of the corpse in ancient times were wont to rest with their burden, and where the officiating minister met it. [Robinson, *DOL*]

corsned A piece of "ordeal bread," by eating which a person accused of crime was allowed to clear himself in certain cases. A prayer was uttered over the morsel to be eaten, that it might choke the person accused if guilty, and the curse was solemnised by marking the corsned with the sign of the cross. Thus the word may be explained from Anglo-Saxon *snoed*, morsel, as signifying . . . the "morsel of the curse." [Wedgwood] SEE *exsufflation*

couchee A visit received about bedtime. [Worcester]

count kin *To count kin with one*, to compare one's pedigree with that of another. It is common for one who has perhaps been spoken of disrespectfully, in regard to his relations, to say of the person who has done so, "I'll *count kin* with him whenever he likes." [Wedgwood]

coup-de-soleil A disease produced by exposure of the head to the rays of the sun. [Stormonth] SEE *crizzles, electric-sunstroke*

court-holy-water Flattery. [Davies] Compliments, faire words, flattering speeches. [Cotgrave] SEE *puzzomous, soft-wind*

court plaster The plaster of which the court ladies made their patches. These patches, worn on the face, were cut into the shapes of crescents, stars, circles, diamonds, hearts, crosses . . .

---

and even . . . a ship in full sail, a château, etc. This ridiculous fashion was in vogue in the reign of Charles I, and in the reign of Anne was employed as the badge of political partisanship. . . . If the patch was on the right cheek, it indicated that the wearer was a Whig; if on the left cheek, a Tory. [Brewer]

cover-slut A long apron used to hide an untidy dress; any clothing slipped on to hide untidiness beneath. [J. Wright] Something to hide sluttishness. [Ogilvie] SEE *mucksluff*

cowfyne A ludicrous term of endearment. [Jamieson] SEE *bellibone, pigsnye, snoutfair*

cow-handed Awkward. [Grose, *DVT*] SEE *thumbassing*

cow's band The band binding the cow to the stake, given in pledge for borrowed money. [Warrack] It was an ancient custom in Dumfrieshire . . . that when a man borrowed money, he gave the *cow's band* in pledge, which was reckoned as legal an obligation as a bill. [Jamieson]

cradle crown In mediaeval England, a fine paid by a priest, in lieu of penance, for fathering a child in his house, and keeping a concubine. [Brewer] SEE *parnel*

cragsman One who climbs *crags*, or cliffs, to procure sea-fowls or their eggs. [Jamieson] SEE *neeze*

cramble To walk ill, as with corns on the feet; to hobble. [Robinson, *GYW*] SEE *noggle*

crample-hamm'd Stiffened in the lower joints. [Holloway] SEE *hipshot*

cramp-ring Ring made out of old coffin-lead, and worn as a preservative against cramp. [Robinson, GMY] Their form was probably not material, but their supposed virtue in preventing the cramp was conferred by solemn consecration on Good Friday, among the ceremonies of that great day. Our kings of the Plantagenet line used to give such rings. [Nares] The superstition continues, though the metal is of necessity changed, few coffins having now hinges of silver. The stranger in Lancashire can be nowhere . . . without seeing . . . what are called "galvanized rings" made of two hoops, one of zinc and the other copper, soldered together. [Harland]

crapulous Surcharged with liquor; sick by intemperence. [Ogilvie] Given to gluttony, over-eating, &c. [Barclay] From Latin *crapulosus*, French *crapuleux*, given to drunkenness. [Worcester] SEE *gillmaw, lust-dieted, nyaffle, vorago*

crastine To put off from day to day. [Coles]

crewdling A cold, dull, inactive and sickly person, whose blood seems to be, as it were . . . *curdling*. [Elworthy]

critical days Wherein the disease comes to its crisis, the odd days and fourteenth, especially. [Coles] SEE *medicinal days*

crizzles The rough, sunburnt places on the face and hands in scorching weather. [Robinson, GWW] SEE *coup-de-soleil, electric-sunstroke*

crobbacking A stomach-ache. [Kirkby]

cronk Sitting or squatting to pass or idle the time away, smoking or gossiping. [Wilkinson] SEE *spermologer*

croodle To snuggle, as a young animal snuggles against its

cronk

mother. [Holland] To creep close together, as children round the fire, or chickens under the hen. [Marshall]

crop-lifting Theft of a standing crop of grain. [Zell]

cruddle To thicken the seminal substance in the womb till it be formed into flesh and bones, as milk is thickened in order to make cheese. [Inspired by] Job: X, 10. [Brown]

cruddy-butter A preparation of butter and cheese, of half each. [Warrack] SEE *butterine*

crulge To cramp oneself by sitting in a crouching attitude. *Scotland, Ireland* [Patterson]

crunkle To . . . creake like a crane. [Cotgrave] SEE *towrus*

crying-cheese Cheese given to neighbors and visitors on the occasion of the birth of a child. [Warrack]

cucking-stool A machine formerly used for the punishment of scolds and brawling women; also a punishment antiently inflicted on brewers and bakers who transgressed the laws, and were, in such a chair or stool, to be ducked and immersed in some muddy or stinking pond. [Also called] a *choaking-stool* because scolds being thus punished are almost choaked with water . . . The Saxons called it *scealping stole*. [Bailey]

cuckoo-ale Ale drunk out of doors to welcome the cuckoo's return. [Halliwell] A singular custom prevails in Shropshire at this period of the year [spring], which is peculiar to that county. As soon as the first cuckoo has been heard, all the labouring classes leave work, if in the middle of the day, and time is devoted to mirth and jollity over what has been called the *Cuckoo Ale*. [Brand]

cucupha A sort of coif or cap, with a double bottom, between which is enclosed a mixture of aromatic powders, having cotton for an excipient. It was formerly used as a powerful cephalic. [Dunglison]

culf The dust and small feathers of a bed which adhere to the clothes of anyone who has lain upon it. [J. Wright] SEE *beggar's velvet*

culliage An ancient custom in Scotland which gave a lord the liberty of lying the first night with his vassal's bride. [Dyche] SEE *maiden-rent*

cumberworld A person so idle, dissolute or deformed as to be a burthen to his friends and to society. [Mackay] SEE *slister, idle-worms*

cupidity Inordinate desire, covetousness, sensuality, lust. [Bailey] Unlawful or unreasonable longing. [Johnson] From Latin *cupiditas*, desire, avidity; *cupio*, I wish, desire, long for. [Wedgwood]

curglaff The shock felt in bathing when one first plunges into the cold water. [Jamieson]

curtain-lecture A reproof given by a wife to her husband in bed. [Johnson] What endless brawls by wives are bred! The curtain-lecture makes a mournful bed. [John Dryden] SEE *clapperclaw, tongue-whaled, xantippe*

cut-fingered A ludicrous term applied to one who gives a short answer, or replies with some degree of acrimony. The idea seems borrowed from the peevish humour manifested when one has cut one's finger. [Jamieson] SEE *waspish*

cut-legs It was the common custom forty years ago, when two carters stopped with their teams at the same public-house, for the men to while away the time while their horses were baiting, to shake hands, stand a pace or two apart, and then lash into one another's legs with their cart-whips, till one called *Hold!* the penalty being, of course, payment for two mugs of ale. [Lowsley]

cutty-stool The cutty-stool is a kind of pillory in a church, erected for the punishment of those who have transgressed in the article of chastity. . . . This seems formed from *cutty, kitty,* a light woman. [Sinclair] SEE *bedswerver, spouse-breach*

cynanthropy Madness caused by the bite of a dog, wherein the patient avoids light and water; or a particular kind of melancholy when men fancy themselves changed into dogs, and imitate their actions. [Bailey] A frenzy which makes a man haunt unfrequented places, with a conceit that he is turned into a dog. [Cotgrave] SEE *loup-garou*

dangwallet Abundantly, excessively, plentifully; an old word. [Bailey] A spendthrift. *Cheshire* [J. Wright]

dansey-headed Giddy, thoughtless. Persons growing giddy from dancing. [Holloway]

daring-glass A mirror used for *daring* larks. [Lyons] Larks were dared or fascinated in various ways. One mode was by mirrors which, I suppose, dazzled and confused them, making it easy to capture them. [Davies]

dark-house A mad house; sometimes a darkened room for confining madmen. [Phin]

darkmans The night. The *child of darkmans*, a bell-man. [Smith]

davering Riding or walking in a dazed condition; [from] *daver*, to wander aimlessly, to go out of one's way from stupor; to wander in mind, become stupid. *Scotland, Northern England* [J. Wright] SEE *roozles*

daw Daw, in common speech, is to awaken; to *be dawed*, to have shaken off sleep, to be fully awakened and to come to one's self out of a deep sleep. [Ray]

day-mare A species of incubus [nightmare] occurring during wakefulness. [Hoblyn]

day-spring The first appearance of light in the morning; the dawn. [Fenning]

dead men's shoes *To wait for dead men's shoes*, to wait for a place till it becomes vacant by the death of the present possessor. This corresponds with the adage, "He goes long barefoot that wears *dead men's shoes*," spoken to them who expect to be some man's heir, to get his place, or his wife, if he should die. [Jamieson]

dead-pay Type of fraud where army officers left the deaths of soldiers unreported so as to appropriate their pay. [T. Wright]

death-hunter Persons who go from village to village, as a burial occurs, carrying small black stools called *buffets,* on which the coffin is rested while the funeral hymn is being sung in the open air, in front of the house where the corpse has lain. These stools are also useful on the way to church, distant, in some cases, several miles. Some carriages have got their public hearse, but this vehicle finds no favour. Its use is objected to on superstitious grounds. [Robinson, GMY]

deathwatch An insect [*Arobium tessellatum*] that makes a tickling noise like that of a watch, and is superstitiously imagined to prognosticate death. [Johnson] SEE *elfmill*

deepmusing Contemplative; lost in thought. [Walker] SEE *brownstudy*

demi-island, demi-isle A peninsula. Used before the word *peninsula* had been introduced into English. [R. Hunter] SEE *seasurrounded*

dendranthopology Study based on the theory that man had sprung from trees. [Davies]

deosculation The act of kissing. [Johnson] SEE *cataglottism, rabbit's-kiss*

devil's smiles Gleams of sunshine among dark clouds, either in the heavens or the captain's face. [Smyth] SEE *Noah's ark, sun-suckers, thwankin*

dew-drink The first allowance of beer to harvest men, before they begin their day's work. [Forby] A draught before breakfast. [Brewer] SEE *harvest-wet*

diaplasticks Medicines which are good for a limb out of place. [Bailey]

dirt-haste A coarse and vulgar term denoting the hurry occasioned by one's losing the power of bowel retention . . . This allusion is not peculiar to Scotland. [Jamieson]

disquixotted Disallusioned. [Mathews]

disvirginare To unmaiden, disvirgin. [Florio]

dittology Double reading, such as divers texts of scripture will admit of. [Phillips]

deosculation

doattee To nod the head when sleep comes on whilst one is sitting up. This action is . . . to be noticed in church. [Elworthy]

dog-draw One of the four causes for which a man may be arrested as a deer-stealer, he being found leading a hound who is pursuing a deer by scent. [Dyche] Where any man hath striken or wounded a wild beast by shooting at him, either with crosse bow or long bow, and is found with a hound or other dogge drawing after him to recover the same; this the old forresters do call *dogge-drawe.* [Manwood] SEE *bloody-hand, yburpananseca*

dogflaws Gusts of rage. [Halliwell]

dog-Latin Barbarous Latin, such as was formerly used by lawyers in their pleadings. Now applied to "medical Latin." [Hotten] Sham Latin; also *kitchen-, bog-, garden-,* or *apothecaries'-Latin.* [Farmer] SEE *cat-Latin, thieves' Latin*

dog's-letter The letter *R,* from its sound; also called *canine letter.* [R. Hunter]

dog's soup Rain water. [Grose, *DVT*] SEE *Adam's ale, water-bewitched*

dole-beer Beer distributed to the poor. [Nares]

double-ribbed Pregnant. [Carr]

double-sib Related both by father and mother. [Jamieson] SEE *gutterblood, queer-gotten, skenchback*

dower-house In Great Britain, a house provided for the residence of a widow after the estate of her husband, with its manor-house, has passed to the heir. [Whitney] SEE *sailors' home*

dowfart, duffart A stupid, dull, soft fellow . . . [From] *dowf,* dull, inactive, heavy, wanting in animation, and *art,* as in braggart. *Scotland* [J.Wright]

dragging-time The twilight time, when young fellows at fairs pull the wenches about. *East Anglia, Sussex* [J.Wright]

draw-gloves A game formerly in vogue for representing words by manipulation of the fingers. [Zell] A sort of game, the particulars of which the learned have not yet discovered . . .

In all the instances, it seems to be a game between lovers. [Nares]

drawing the nail Absolving oneself of a vow. In Cheshire, two or more persons would agree to do something, or to abstain from something, say drinking beer, and they would go into a wood and register their vow by driving a nail into a tree, swearing to keep their vow as long as that nail remained in the tree. If they repented of their vow, some or all of the party went and drew out the nail, whereupon the vow was cancelled. [Brewer]

dream-hole One of the slits or loopholes left in the walls of steeples, towers, barns, &c., to allow the sound of the bells to escape, and to admit air and light. [J. Wright] From Anglo-Saxon *dreám*, music. [Robinson, GMY]

drenching-horn A horn into which the *drench*, a draught or potion for horses or cattle, is put as a convenient means of pouring it down the animal's throat; from Anglo-Saxon *drenc-horn*. [Jackson]

dress-lodger A prostitute who is lent dresses by the owner of an immoral house. [J. Wright] The dress-lodger gets as much money from her man as she can succeed in abstracting, and is given a small percentage on what she obtains by her employer. [Mayhew] SEE *laced-mutton*

drink tobacco To smoke; formerly a common phrase . . . In *The Roaring Girl*, one of the personages says of some tobacco, "This will serve to drink at my chamber." [Nares]

drizzen To low as a cow or ox. The term seems rather to denote a low mournful sound applied to a lazy person groaning over his work. [Jamieson]

droll-booth A travelling theater; a place of exhibition for puppet-shows. [R. Hunter]

drowning the miller Adding too much water to wine or spirits; from the term when too much water has been put into a bowl of flour. [Smyth] SEE *six-water grog*, *water-bewitched*

drum-roll payment Not to pay at all. No soldier can be arrested for debt when on the march. [Brewer]

droll-booth

drunkard's-cloak In the time of the commonwealth, the magistrates of Newcastle punished . . . drunkards by making them carry a tub with holes in the sides for the arms to pass through, called the *drunkard's-cloak*, through the streets of that town. [Hazlitt]

dry diet A term denoting restriction in the amount of alimentary fluids. By *dry treatment* is signified the total abstinence from liquids. [Hoblyn] SEE *banting*

dudman A scarecrow made of old garments. [Mackay] SEE *rattle-bladder*

duffifie [In] Aberdeen, to lay a bottle on its side for some time, after its contents have been poured out, that it may be completely drained of the few drops remaining. Elsewhere, one is said to "make the bottle confess." [Jamieson]

Dutch auction An auction in which the auctioneer starts with a high price, which he gradually lowers till he meets with a bidder. [R. Hunter]

dwang To oppress with too much labour; to harrass, worry; hence, *dwanged*, bowed down, decrepit. *Scotland* [J. Wright]

dwizzen To shrink and dry up; to have a parched appearance, as withered fruit, or the skin of old people. A skinny-looking person is *dwizzen-faced*. [Robinson, GMY]

eagle-stone A variety of iron ore, so called from the belief that it was found in the nest of the eagle, where it was supposed to prevent [its] eggs from becoming rotten. [Hoblyn] This stone was formerly supposed to facilitate delivery if bound on the thigh, and to prevent abortion if bound on the arm. [Dunglison] A fossil which rattles due to the presence of a bit of debris found within. It was supposed that eagles sought these for their nests and could not raise healthy young without one. It was used as a charm by expectant mothers to prevent abortion. [Johnson]

earguards Small side-whiskers once favoured by men who worked in clouds of dust in sheepyards. [Baker]

ear-rent Payment made by mutilation or loss of the ears. [R. Hunter]

eassin To desire the male. In this sense, a cow is said to be *eass-enin*. Metaphorically used to express a strong desire of any kind. . . . In the parish of Calder, the country people call [a] plant [*Morsus diaboli*] *eastningwort*, which they affirm makes cowes come to bulling when they get it amongst their meat. [Jamieson] SEE *breem, clicketing, towrus*

eattocks Dainties, sweets, etc. *Scotland* [J. Wright] SEE *rere-banket, sculsh*

egg-wife-trott An easy jog, such a speed as farmers' wives carry their eggs to the market. [Carr] SEE *midwife-gallop*

electric-sunstroke An effect resembling that of sunstroke, sometimes experienced by those who have been for a long time exposed to intense electric light. [R. Hunter] SEE *coup-de-soleil*

elflocks Knots of hair twisted by elves. [Walker] It was supposed to be a spiteful amusement of Queen Mab and her subjects to twist the hair of human creatures, or manes and tails of horses, into hard knots which it was not fortunate to untangle. [Nares] SEE *tazzled, witch's-stirrups*

elfmill The sound made by a worm in the timber of a house, supposed by the vulgar to be preternatural. [Jamieson] A sound like that of a mill, heard when listening at a hole in the ground. [J. Wright] I have often listened to the most celebrated of the elf-mills, and the sound is that of running water. [Nicolson] SEE *deathwatch*

empasm In pharmacy, a powder sprinkled on the body to correct some ill smell. [Fenning] From Greek *empasso*, to sprinkle. [R. Hunter] SEE *carfumish, natkin, odor of sanctity*

encraty Mastery over the senses; abstinence from pleasures of sense; self-control, as experienced in fasting and continence, especially the latter. [Whitney]

enneagon A figure of nine angles. [Johnson] SEE *chilihedron, umstroke*

entaticon A plaster to excite venereal inclination. [J. Coxe]

enthasy A soft, quiet . . . passage out of this world. [Bailey] SEE *placeparted, sleepaway*

equinecessary Needful in the same degree. [Johnson]

erotomania The melancholy of lovers. [J. Coxe]

errhines Medicines to put up the nostrils to cleanse the head . . . or to enliven the spirits. [Bailey]

errorist One who errs, or encourages and propagates error. [Whitney]

Eve's scork The larynx, *pomum Adami*. [Jackson]

exflunct To overcome or beat thoroughly; to use up completely. [Mathews]

exlex An outlaw; [from] Latin *ex*, out, away, and *lex*, law. [R. Hunter]

exophagy A custom of certain cannibal tribes, prohibiting the eating of persons of their own tribe. [From] Greek *exo*, outside, and *phagy*, eat. [Whitney]

expeditate A word usual in the Forest Laws, signifying to remove the balls of dogs' feet or, to cut off by the skin, the three claws of the forefoot on the right side for the preservation of the king's game. Every one that kept any great dogs not expeditated did forfeit to the king three shillings and four pence. . . . From *ex* and *pes,* to unfoot. [Blount, G]

exsufflation A kind of exorcism performed by blowing and spitting at the evil spirit . . . Exsufflate was an old ecclesiastical term for the form of renouncing the devil in the baptism of catachumens, when the candidate was commanded to turn to the west and thrice sufflate Satan. [Lyons] SEE *corsned*

extramundane The infinite empty space, which is by some supposed to be extended beyond the bounds of the universe, and in which there is nothing at all. [Bailey] SEE *firmament*

extranean An outsider, stranger; one not belonging to a household . . . In the grammar school at Aberdeen, the extranean was one who had not gone through the regular curriculum from the lowest to the highest classes, but had come from other schools for the last quarter in order to get a final drill or finishing touch before going to compete for the university bursaries or scholarships. *Scotland* [J. Wright]

eye-bite To bewitch with a malign influence whatever the eye glances upon. The dread of this malign influence was not unknown to the Romans. [Carr] The Irish at one time believed that their children and cattle could be "eyebitten," that is, bewitched by an evil eye, and that the *eyebiter,* or witch, could rhyme them to death. [Brewer] SEE *ratt-rime, sheep's-eye*

eyeshot, sight-shot Sight, glance, view. [Johnson] *Out of sightshot,* out of sight; *ear-shot* is common. [Davies] *Eye-reach,*

eye-waiter

the range or reach of the eye; extent of vision. [Whitney]
SEE *tongue-shot*

eye-waiter A servant who performs duties diligently only while his master looks on. [Davies]

fabulosity The quality of being fabulous. [Whitney] The quality of dealing in falsehood, or telling lies. [Fenning]

faffle Said of work which occupies much time, the results not being satisfactory or commensurate with the labour and time expended on it. [Dickinson]

fairy-money Money given by fairies which, according to popular belief, was said to turn into withered leaves or rubbish after some time . . . A term sometimes applied to found money, from the notion that it was dropped by a good fairy where the favored mortal would find it. [Lyons] SEE *pelf*

faleste A capital punishment inflicted on a malefactor on the seashore, by laying him bound on the sands till the next full tide carried him away. [From Norman] *falese,* sands, rocks, cliffs. [Bouvier]

falling-band A necktie. *Yorkshire* [J. Wright]

falling-weather Rain, snow or hail. [R. Hunter] SEE *by planets, peppering shower*

fangast A marriageable maid. *Norfolk* [Grose, PG]

fanticles, fern-tickles Freckles on the skin resembling the seeds of the *fern*, freckled with fern, quite like small *ticks* . . . Ferns are frequently the receptacle of ticks, of which *tickles* may be considered a diminutive. [Carr] These are popularly accounted for as the marks made by the spurting of milk from the mother's breast, inevitably occasioned, so that a face may be marred that is "over bonny." [Robinson, GMY]

farded Painted, embellished; [from] French *farder*, to paint, colour, trick up with false beauties. *Scotland* [J. Wright] SEE *redubbers*

fasting-spittle The spittle of a fasting man, supposed to possess magical powers of healing. *Yorkshire* [J. Wright] A cure for ringworm: Put a new shilling three times round the crook, spit a fastin on it, and with it rub the affected parts. Some, in addition, dropped the shilling through the patient's shirt before rubbing with it. [Gregor]

fatherbetter Surpassing one's father, in any respect. This term is very ancient; from Icelandic *faudrbetringr*, and is also inverted, *betur fedrungar*. [Jamieson]

fattening and battening A toast of a child's fattening and thriving given at its baptism in private, when the bread, cheese and whisky customarily are partaken of. [Warrack]

fatty-cakes Hot cakes kneaded with lard or dripping[s], oven-

fattening and battening

baked and served to tea. They are very tasty and require little butter, being greasy enough themselves. [Wilkinson] SEE
browis, sowl

feague To put ginger up a horse's fundament, and formerly, as it
is said, a live eel, to make him lively and carry his tail well.
It is said a forfeit is incurred by any horse-dealer's servant
who shall shew a horse without first feaguing him. Feague is
used figuratively for encouraging or spiriting one up. [Grose,
DVT] SEE *horse chaunter*

featherdriver One who cleanses feathers by whisking them about. [Johnson] One who beats feathers to make them light and loose. [Webster]

feff A bad smell; a stench. Applied by mothers to infants troubled by wind. *Scotland* [J. Wright] SEE *carfumish, odor of sanctity, natkin*

felth The power of feeling in the fingers. [Mackay]

ferry-whisk Great bustle, haste. *Yorkshire* [Halliwell] SEE *fluck-adrift, hurrion*

fiddlers' green The place where sailors expect to go when they die. It's a place of fiddling, dancing, rum, and tobacco, and is undoubtedly the "Land of Cocaigne" mentioned in medieval manuscripts. [Hotten] A sailors' elysium (situate on the hither and cooler side of hell) of wine, women and song. [Farmer]

figging-law A little boy put in a window to hand out goods to the diver. [Grose, *DVT*] SEE *little snakesman, moon curser, Tyburn-blossom*

fighting-water Casks filled and placed on the decks, expressly for use in action. When the head was broken in [cask was opened] vinegar was added to prevent too much being taken by one man. [Smyth]

fillemot A colour like that of a faded leaf; from French *fueille-mort*, a dead leaf. [Bailey]

fingerfull A pinch, small quantity. *Scotland* [J. Wright] SEE *pugil*

finger-poke The finger of a glove, cut off to place on a burnt or

firmament

injured finger whilst undergoing treatment. [Wilkinson] SEE *caddis*

firmament A term anciently used to signify the *eighth heaven*, or sphere in which the fixed stars were placed. It was called the eighth heaven because of the seven spheres of the planets which it surrounds. The firmament was supposed to have two motions, one from east to west, round about the poles of the ecliptic, and the other and opposite motion from west to east. [Zell] SEE *extramundane*, *planet-ruler*, *primovant*, *stelliscript*

fishfag Originally a Billingsgate fishwife; now any scolding, vixenish, foul-mouthed woman. [Hotten] SEE *tongue-whaled, xantippe*

five wits It has been thought that the five senses were originally meant by it, but the expression was also used when no reference to the senses, properly so called, could be had. . . . The *five wits*, properly enumerated were, "common wit, imagination, fantasy, estimation and memory." [Nares]

flag-fallen Out of employment, from flags being exhibited on the roofs of play-houses when there were performances at them. [R. Hunter]

flamfoo A gaudily dressed female, one whose chief pleasure consists of dress. Perhaps from *flam*, an illusory pretext, and *foye*, what excites disgust. This term, however, seems to be the same with Old English *flamefew*, "the moonshine in the water." [Jamieson]

flap-dragon A [pastime] in which they catch raisins out of burning brandy and, extinguishing them by closing the mouth, eat them; from *dragon*, supposed to breathe fire. [Johnson] A small substance, such as a plum or candle-end, set afloat in a cup of spirits, and then to be set on fire, to be snatched by the mouth and swallowed. This was a common amusement in former times, but now nearly obsolete. *Flap-dragon* was also a cant term for the *lues venerea*. [Halliwell]

flarting Mocking, jeering. *Northumberland* [J. Wright]

flathers Rubbish; [from] *flath*, filth, dirt, ordure. [Mackay] SEE *pelf*

flattybouch One who goes from place to place in a van during the summer months, but lives in a house during the winter. A gypsy term. *Wiltshire* [J. Wright] SEE *palliard, sorn*

flatuosity Windiness, fullness of wind. [Blount, G] SEE *thorough cough*

flepper The under lip. [Carr] SEE *swine-greun*

fleshment Excitement from a first success. From the verb *to flesh*, which in the sixteenth and seventeenth centuries meant to give a hawk, falcon [or] hound some of the flesh of the first game killed, to excite it to further hunting. [Shipley]

fleshquake A tremor of the body; a word formed by [Ben] Jonson in imitation of *earthquake*. [Johnson]

flesh-spade A fingernail. [Davies]

flesh-tailor A surgeon. [R. Hunter]

fleshy pannicle The fourth covering of the body from head to foot. [Coles]

flizzen To laugh with the whole of the face; *flizzy*, applied to those who are inclined to laugh at little. [Robinson, GMY] To laugh sarcastically. [Carr]

flobbage This seems to signify phlegm, *flabby* or flaccid stuff from the throat. [Jamieson]

flodder To disfigure [the face] in consequence of weeping. It contains an allusion to the marks left on the banks of a river by an inundation; [from] Swedish *flod-a*, to overflow. [Jamieson] SEE *begrutten*

flonker Anything very large or outrageous. [Kirkby]

flothery Slovenly but attempting to be fine and showy. [Halliwell]

fluckadrift A haste, hurry. *Shetland and Orkney Islands* [J. Wright] SEE *ferry-whisk, hurrion*

flurch A multitude, a great many; spoken of things, not persons, as a *flurch* of strawberries. [Ray]

flurn To show contempt by looks; to scorn. [Brogden]

flychter To run with outstretched arms, like a tame goose half-flying; applied to children when running to those to whom they are much attached. [Jamieson]

fogorner One who expels people from their dwellings. [T. Wright]

foof Of a dog, to howl or whine in a melancholic manner. *Ireland* [J. Wright]

foot-ale Money paid for liquor by a newcomer into a manufactory, to his fellow work-men. The word may be classed with *bride-ales, church-ales, clerk-ales, give-ales, lamb-ales, leet-ales, midsummer-ales, scot-ales, whitsun-ales*, all mentioned by Nares. None of these terms are heard in the district to which this term relates, foot-ales being the only survivor of the whole brotherhood. [J. Hunter] When a young horse gets its first shoes, it is customary for the smith and owner to drink the *foot-yell*. [Heslop] A fine paid by a young man when found courting out of his own district. [Dickinson] SEE *audit ale, cockwalk, outcumlins*

footmanship The art or faculty of a runner. [Johnson]

forehead-cloth A bandage used by ladies to prevent wrinkles. [Nares]

forestall To buy victuall or other merchandise by the way before it come to the faire or market; to sell it againe at a dearer price. [Bullokar] This was an offence at law up till 1844. [Lyons]

forswunk Utterly worn out with *swink*, or hard labor. [Mackay] From Low German *swunken*, to sway to and fro, as a tree under the impulse of a violent wind. [Wedgwood] SEE *ramfeezled*

fratchy Quarrelsome. [Mackay] SEE *nattlesome*

freed-stool A seat or chair in churches near the altar, to which offenders fled for sanctuary as their last and most sacred refuge. [Halliwell]

freemartin When a cow happens to bring forth two calves, one of them a male, the other a female, the former is a perfect animal, but the latter is incapable of propagation, and is well known to farmers under the denomination of a *freemartin*. [Bewick]

freemason's-cup A drink made of ale, especially Scotch ale, and sherry in equal parts, with the addition of some brandy, sugar and nutmeg. [Whitney]

fribbler A trifler; a fribbler is one who professes rapture for a woman, and dreads her consent. [Johnson]

frippery A shop where old clothes are sold. [Phin] Worn-out clothes; then the place where old clothes are sold, or such faded finery as is sold by dealers in old clothes. [From] French *friper*, to rub, to wear to rags . . . The origin seems a form of *frip*, related to the *fric* in Latin *fricare*, to rub. [Wedgwood]

froonce To go about in an active, bustling manner. *Yorkshire* [J. Wright]

fubbery Deceit; deception; cheating. [From] *fub*, to shift. [Worcester]

fugleman A corporal, or active adept, who exhibits the time for each [military] motion at the word of command, to enable soldiers, marines and small-arm men to act simultaneously. [Smyth] Hence, one who takes the initiative in any movement, and sets an example for others to follow; particularly one who acts as the mouthpiece or in the interest of others; a ringleader. [Whitney]

fulham An old cant word for false dice, named from Fulham, a suburb of London which, in the reign of Queen Elizabeth, was the most notorious place for *black-legs* [sharpers] in all England. Those made to throw the high numbers, from five to twelve, were called *high fulhams* and those to throw the low numbers, the low from ace to four, *low fulhams*. [Lyons]

furole A little blaze of fire appearing by night at sea on sailyards which whirls and leaps in a moment from place to place. It is sometimes the forerunner of a storm . . . and is thought to forebode shipwreck. [Bailey] SEE *sea-dog*

fuzzle To make fuzzy, or indistinct with drink. To *fossle, vossle*, to entangle, to confute business. [From] Low German *fusslig*, just tipsy enough to speak indistinctly. [Wedgwood]

gaberlunzie A mendicant; a poor guest who cannot pay for his entertainment. A contraction for *gaberlunzie-man*, from Scotch *gaberlunzie*, a wallet, and that compounded of a contraction of . . . *gaberdine* and *lunzie*, a Scotch form of *loin*, a wallet resting on the loins. [Lyons] SEE *walleteer*

gall of bitterness The bitterest grief; extreme affliction. The ancients taught that grief and joy were subject to the gall, affection to the heart, knowledge to the kidneys, anger to the bile, and courage or timidity to the liver. The gall of bitterness means the bitter center of bitterness, as the "heart of hearts" means the innermost recesses of the heart, or affections. [Brewer]

gallopped-beer Small beer made for present drinking, by simply boiling small quantities of malt and hops together in a kettle; so called from being made in haste, *gallopped*, as it were, into beer. [Holloway]

gallywow A man destitute of the power of begetting children. *Cornwall* [J. Wright]

gandermonth, gandermoon The month in which a man's wife is confined [following childbirth]. *To go a-gandering*, to gallant during this season. [T. Wright] Literally the month in which a goose is sitting, and the gander looks lost and wanders vacantly about. [Holland]

gapesnest A wonderment, a strange sight. Fit only to be stared at, as some strange, uncommon creature; a *gazingstock*. [Elworthy] SEE *gazingstock, pointing-stock*

gardyloo, jordeloo A cry which servants in the higher stories of Edinburgh give, after ten o'clock at night, when they throw their dirty water, &c. from the windows; hence, also used to denote the contents of the vessel. From French *gardez l'eau,* save yourselves from water. French *gare*, indeed, is a term used to give warning, as [Cotgrave's] *gare le heurt,* "the voice of those that drived horned beasts, [be]warre [of] hornes." [Jamieson]

gazingstock An object of public notice, contempt and abhorrence. [Fenning] SEE *pointing-stock, talkingstock*

gazooly To be constantly uttering laments . . . [From] French *gazouiller,* to warble, as a young bird when it first begins or learns to sing. *Cornwall* [J. Wright]

geloscopy Divination by means of laughter. [Worcester]

gardyloo

geo-graffy A beverage made by seamen of burnt biscuit boiled in water. [Smyth]

giggle-trot A woman who marries when she is far advanced in life is said *to take the giggle-trot*. [Jamieson]

gill-gatherers One who gathers leeches [for medical use] in the marshes; from Gaelic and Irish *gael*, a leech. [J. Wright]

gillmaw A glutton; a voracious eater. [Warrack] SEE *kedge-belly, lust-dieted, nyaffle, papelard*

gill-wheep *To get the gill-wheep,* to be jilted. This may be from the same fountain as English *jilt* . . . from the Swedish *gyll-a*, to deceive, conjoined with *wheep*, as denoting something unexpected. [Jamieson] To be always grinning and laughing. *Derbyshire* [Grose, *PGS*]

glad-warbling Singing or walking joyfully. [R. Hunter]

glaums Instruments used by horse-gelders when gelding. [Mactaggart] Pincers; [from] *glaum*, to grope, especially in the dark . . . It most generally denotes a feeble and ineffectual attempt, as that of an infant who begins to grasp ["glom onto"] objects. [Jamieson]

glee-dream Merriment caused by music; minstrelsy. [From] Anglo-Saxon *gléo*, joy, and *dréam*, music. [R. Hunter]

glister A liquor made sometime of sodden flesh, sometime with decoction of hearbes or other thinges, which by a pipe is conveyed into the lower parts of the body. It is written that the use hereof was first learned from a bird in Egypt called *Ibis*, much like unto a storke, which bird doth often with her bill open her hinder parts, when nature of her selfe dooth not expell what is needefull. [Bullokar]

gloppened Surprised. [Thoresby] SEE *blutterbunged*

glorg To work in some dirty business. [Jamieson]

glory-hole A place for rubbish or odds and ends, as a housemaid's cupboard, or a lumber room. [Dartnell] SEE *flathers*

glox The sound of liquids when shaken in a barrel. [Halliwell] SEE *squiggle*

gludder The sound of a body falling among mire. [Jamieson]

glunch To frown. [Mackay]

goatmilker A kind of owl, so called from sucking goats. [Johnson]

goblocks Large mouthfulls. *Yorkshire* [Grose, *SPG*]

gold-beater's skin The *intestinum rectum* of an ox, which goldbeaters lay between the leaves of their metal while they beat it [into sheets], whereby the membrane is reduced thin and made fit to apply to cuts or small fresh wounds, as is now the common practice. [Johnson] SEE *link-hides, pudding-leather*

gombeen-man, gombeen-woman A village money-lender, usurer. *Ireland, Isle of Man* [J. Wright]

goodman's-croft A strip of ground or corner of a field formerly left untilled in Scotland, in the belief that unless some such place were left, the spirit of evil would damage the crop. [R. Hunter]

gospel gossip One who is over-zealous in running among his neighbours to lecture on religious subjects. [Ogilvie]

gowl To weep in anger more than in sorrow, sulkily and vindictively, rather than in penitence. [Mackay] SEE *begrutten*

gowpen A handful. The hollow of the hand when contracted in a semicircular form to receive anything. To lift or lade out, with the hands spread out and placed together. [R. Hunter] SEE *yeepsen*

grace-drink A drink taken after grace at the close of a meal. [Warrack]

gramarye Magic. This is evidently from French *grammaire*, grammar, as the vulgar formerly believed that the *black art* was scientifically taught, and indeed ascribed a considerable degree of knowledge, especially in [medicine] and almost everything pertaining to experimental philosophy, to magic. . . . The learned editor [Bishop Percy] gives materially the same view of the origin of the term, "In those dark and ignorant ages, when it was thought a high degree of learning to read and write, he who made a little further progress in literature might well pass for a conjurer or magician." [Jamieson]

grammar-folk Educated people. [Warrack]

grampuse A corruption of *gran pisce* [French for *large fish*]. An animal of the cetacean or whale tribe, distinguished by the large pointed teeth with which both jaws are armed . . .

greenboarded

Blowing the grampuse: sluicing [dousing] a person with water, especially practised on him who skulks, or sleeps on his watch. [Smyth]

grannows Streaks of dirt left in clothes from bad washing; the term is chiefly applied to body-linen. [Jackson]

gratulate To rejoice. [Florio]

gravel-blind Worse than *sand-blind*. [Phin]

greasy tongue A "greasy tongue" is said of one who insinuates with soft, flattering words. [Wilkinson] SEE *papelard*

great-hundred One hundred and twenty nails, tacks, deals, etc. [Ogilvie]

greenboarded To *be greenboarded* is when a servant is [brought] into the drawing-room, or elsewhere, before the master or mistress, to account for any misdoings. [Robinson, *DOL*]

green gown A tousel in the new-mown hay. To "give one a green gown" sometimes means to go beyond the bounds of innocent play. [Brewer] A throwing of young lasses on the grass and kissing them. [B.E.] *To have, get,* or *give one's greens:* to enjoy, procure, or confer the sexual favour. Said indifferently of both sexes. [Farmer]

grimgribber A lawyer. Also, the technical jargon used by a lawyer. [Halliwell]

grinning match The grinning match is performed by two or more persons endeavouring to exceed each other in the distortion of their features, every one of them having his head thrust through a horse's collar. [Strutt] SEE *smoking match*

groaning malt A strong ale brewed for the gossips who attend at the birth of a child, and for those who come to offer to a husband congratulations at the auspicious event. [Brewer]

ground-mail Duty paid for the right of having a corpse interred in a churchyard. [Jamieson] SEE *restial*

grufeling Closely wrapped up and comfortable in a lying posture; used in ridicule. [Warrack]

gryphus A sort of forceps like the beak of a griffin. [Blancard] SEE *pullikins*

gubbertushed Having projecting teeth. [Whitney]

guessive Conjectural. [Worcester]

guddle To catch trout by groping with the hands under the stones or banks of a stream; to dabble as a duck. Used of children, to play in the gutters, mud or puddles; to do work of a dirty or greasy nature. [Warrack]

gumbled Awakening in the morning, the eyes are said to be *gumbled*. [Halliwell]

gun-stones Cannon-balls of stone, used in former times as missles. Even after the introduction of iron shot for heavy artillery, the name *gunstone* was retained in the sense of "bullet." [Phin]

gutterblood Persons are said to be *gutterblood* who have been brought up in the immediate neighbourhood of each other. [Jamieson]

gynacomastax A tuft of hair at the upper part of a woman's secrets; from this, some take their estimate of the temperament of the womb and the testicles. [Blancard] SEE *merkin*

gyromancy A kind of divination said to have been practised

gyrovagues

by walking round in a circle or ring till the performer fell from dizziness, the manner of his fall being interpreted with reference to characters or signs previously placed about the ring, or in some such way. [Whitney] SEE *alectromantia*

gyrovagues Vagabonds who strolled about from one monastery to another, gratifying too freely their inclinations and appetites. [Rankin] SEE *whiffinger*

gyst-ale In Lancashire we find the term *gyst-ale*, which seems to be one of the corruptions of *disguising*, as applied to mumming. . . . Gyst-ale, or *guisin* . . . was celebrated in Eccles with much rustic splendor at the termination of the marling [fertilizing] season, when the villagers, with a "king" at their head, walked in procession with garlands, to which silver plate was attached, which was contributed by the principal gentry in the neighbourhood. [Hampson]

haggard eye A physiognomy [countenance] in which there is, at once, an expression of madness and terror. [Dunglison] The deformity is commonly the effect of a bad education, from allowing children to look angry at those who contradict them, or refuse to give them everything they ask. A prudent governess will check the haughty temper of a child which a foolish mother gives way to. When a child sees himself encouraged in their humours, he becomes more proud, haughty and ill-natured. He looks upon all the world, and even his own mother, with a disdainful air. [Andry] *Haggard*, any thing wild or irreclaimable. [Johnson]

haggersnash A spiteful person. *Ayrshire* [J. Wright]

hair-wreath A wreath made of human hair fashioned into artificial flowers, and suitably mounted and framed to hang on the wall as an ornament. [Mathews]

haimsucken The crime of beating or assaulting a person in his own house. [Tayler]

handfasting A sort of marriage. A fair was at one time held in Dumfriesshire, at which a young man was allowed to pick out a female companion to live with him. They lived together for twelve months, and if they both liked the arrangement, were man and wife. This sort of contract was common among the Romans and Jews, and is not unusual in the East even now. [Brewer] SEE *living tally*

hart royal If the king or queen hunt [a stag] and he escape, then he is called a *hart royal;* and if by such hunting he be chased out of the forest, proclamation is commonly made in the places adjacent that in the regard of the pastime the beast has afforded the king and queen, none shall hurt or hinder him from returning to the forest. [Blount, *LD*] If the king or queen make proclamation for his safe return, he was called a *hart royal proclaimed*. [Halliwell]

harvest-wet A beer frolic at the commencement of harvest. *Norfolk* [J. Wright] SEE *dew-drink*

haspenald A tall youth, betwixt a man and a boy, having shot up like an *aspen, ald* being a diminutive. [Carr]

hastener A long funnel-shaped tin vessel for warming "drink" quickly. When used for this purpose, it is put *into* the fire, not *upon* it, as a sauce pan would. [Jackson]

hat-worship, hat-honor Respect shown by taking off the hat;

a term used by the early . . . Quakers, who refused to pay this token of respect. [Whitney] SEE *off-capped, borrower's cap*

health-lift An apparatus for exercising the muscles by raising a weight by a direct upward lift. It is sometimes so arranged, by means of levers, that the body of a person lifting serves as the weight being lifted. [Whitney]

heart of grace To *take the heart of grace*, or *pluck up the heart of grace*, to be of good heart . . . As a stag in good condition was in hunting language called a *hart of grease*, to pluck up a good heart seems to have been punningly converted into plucking up, or taking a hart of grease, corrupted, when the joke was no longer understood, into *heart of grace*. [Wedgwood]

heart-quakes Tremblings of the heart. [Nares]

heart's attorney The tongue. *Merchant of Venice* [Dyce]

hedge-creep A party of youths will make it up amongst themselves to . . . follow two lovers along the walks which they frequent, but on the other side of a hedge or wall, for the purpose of listening to their conversation, which is supposed to be productive of a high degree of fun. . . . The half-dozen of them who may be engaged . . . put off their shoes and stockings, holding them in one hand as they creep cautiously along, one behind the other. [Robinson, *DOL*] SEE *shimshank*

heel-taps Liquor left on the bottoms of glasses after drinking. [Long] SEE *all sorts*

henfare A fine for flight, imposed upon one accused of murder. Apparently from Middle English *henne*, hence, and *fare*, going. Skinner has it as *hinefar*, explaining it as the flight or desertion of a servant [or] *hind*. [Whitney]

hidegild A price or ransome paid to save one's skin from [a] beating . . . From the Saxon *hide*, the skin, and *gild*, the price by which [a person] redeemed his skin, that is, redeemed it from being whipp'd . . . *Vel hidgildum*, Let him pay for his skin, by which payment he is to be excused from whipping. [Blount, *LD*]

higgle To effect by slow degrees. The poor often talk of *higgling up a pig*, that is of buying and fattening it up by means of small savings. [Holloway]

hippospadians Monstrous persons that abuse themselves with a horse. [Blount, G]

hippuris Disorders proceeding from much riding, as debility and weeping of the genitals. [J. Coxe]

hipshot Sprained or dislocated in the hip. [Browne] SEE *cramp-ple-hamm'd*

hog-mutton The meat of a year-old sheep. From the Scotch dialect word *hog*, a sheep that has not lost its first fleece. [Taylor]

hoined Fatigued, oppressed. This may possibly come from the Anglo-Saxon *hine*, a servant, who was put to great hardships in doing the lord's work. If so, to be *ill-hoin'd* means to be made a great slave of. [Watson]

holus-bolus All at a gulp; altogether. A vulgarism formed from *whole* and *bolus*, a pill. [Lyons]

holy-dabbies Cakes of shortbread, formerly used as communion-bread. [Warrack]

holy laugh A laugh by one in a state of religious hysteria or fervor. [Mathews]

hornbook Leaf of paper containing the alphabet, often with the addition of the ten digits, some elements of spelling, and the Lord's Prayer, protected by a thin plate of translucent horn, and mounted on a tablet of wood, with a projecting piece for a handle. [Onions] SEE *abcedarian*

horn-thumb A thimble of horn worn on the thumb by cutpurses for resisting the edge of a knife in cutting. [Skeat]

horse-boat, team boat A ferry-boat propelled by horses working in a treadmill. [Whitney] The *team boat* . . . is sixty-two feet long and forty-two feet wide, and propelled by eight horses. [Mathews]

horse chaunter A dealer who takes worthless horses to country fairs and disposes of them by artifice. He is generally an unprincipalled fellow, and will put in a glass eye, fill a beast with shot, plug him with ginger [suppositories], or in fact do anything so that he sells to advantage. [Hotten] SEE *feague*

houseleek A plant, so called from growing on the walls or outside roofs of houses. [Fenning] It was thought formerly, and the idea is perhaps not entirely extinct, that if the herb, *houseleek*, did grow on the house-top, the same house is never stricken with lightning or thunder. It is still common in many parts of England to plant the herb upon the tops of cottage houses. [Hazlitt]

hove To take shelter; hence, *hovel*, a sheltering place. [Leigh]

howgates In what manner. *Yorkshire, Lincolnshire* [J. Wright]

huchet A huntsman's horn, from whence comes the word *hue*, cry, clamour. [Bouvier] SEE *hunt's-up*

humming Strong, as applied to drink. Extra strong ale is often characterized as "humming October," maybe from its effect on heads not quite so strong. [Hotten] *Humming ale*, strong liquor that froths well and causes a *humming* in the head of the drinker. [Brewer] SEE *tankard of October*

hunt's-up A morning song, or a tune played on the horn, under the windows of sportsmen to arouse them. [R. Hunter] SEE *aubades, huchet*

hunt the whistle A romping game in which a blinded person has a whistle fastened to him. The other players blow this from time to time, and the blinded one tries to catch the blower. [Davies]

hurple To shrug or stick up the back as an animal does in inclement weather when standing under a hedge. [Atkinson] To shrug up the neck and creep along the streets with a shivering sensation of cold, as an ill-clad person may do on a winter's morning. [Robinson, *DOL*]

hurrion A slut. So called from *hurrying on* things, or doing them so hastily and carelessly that they are not well done. [Watson] SEE *ferry-whisk, fluckadrift*

hydromania A species of melancholy or mental disease, under the influence of which the sufferers are led to commit suicide by drowning. It frequently accompanies the last stages of the disease called *pellegra*. [Lyons] SEE *calenture*

hylden A term of contempt; a great, foul, hulky, filthy creature such as a butcher or hangman. *Gloucestershire* [J. Wright] SEE *cag-mag*

iatromathematique A physician and mathematician . . . that cures in a mathematical way. [Coles] SEE *arithmetician*

ice-anchor An anchor with one arm, used for securing whales to ice floes. [Ogilvie]

idle-worms Worms bred in the fingers of lazy girls, an ancient notion alluded to by Shakespeare [in] *Romeo and Juliet:* "*Not half so big as a round little worm, Pricked from the lazy finger of a maid.*" [Halliwell] It was supposed, and the notion was probably encouraged for the sake of promoting female industry, that when maidens were idle, worms bred in their fingers. . . . To be *sick of the idles,* to be lazy. [Nares] SEE *causey-webs*

illiack passion Wind in the small guts. [Coles] A kind of nervous colick, whose seat is the illeum, whereby that gut is

twisted, or one part enters the cavity of the part immediately below or above. [Walker] SEE *bowelhive, thorough
cough*

incalescence A growing warm and lusty. [Coles] SEE *cupidity*

inch-meal Gradually; by inches or small degrees; [from] Anglo-
Saxon *mael*, a piece. [Donald] A piece an inch long. [John-
son] An example of the modern use of *meal* in this sense is
seen in *piece-meal; limb-meal*, limb by limb. [Phin]

incubus A devil who has carnal knowledge of a [sleeping]
woman, under the shape of a man. [Bailey] The vulgar
thinke it some spirit, but the phisitions affirme it to bee a
naturall disease caused by humours undigested in the stomacke which, fuming up to the braine, doe there trouble the
animall spirits, stopping their passage into the sinews so
that the body cannot moove. [Bullokar] SEE *succubus*

index-learning Superficial knowledge, such as may be gained
from the cursory perusal of a book, or a study of its index.
[R. Hunter]

inexpressibles Trousers or breeches . . . an article of dress not
to be mentioned in polite circles. [Whitney] *Unutterables,
unmentionables, unwhisperables* [also *indescribables, unmentionables*, and *inexplicables*] or *sit upons*, trousers, the nether
garments. All affected terms, having their origins in a most
unpleasant squeamishness. [Hotten]

infradig Below or unworthy of one's dignity, character or position; [from] Latin *infra dignitatem*. [R. Hunter]

inkhorn Any vessel which contains ink; properly applied to a

inkhorn

case made of horn, wherein ink, pens and wafers are contained. [Fenning] It was the custom for persons much employed in writing to carry ink, pens, &c. in a horn which could be attached to the person . . . [hence] *inkhorn terms,* studied expressions that savour of the inkhorn. A very favorite expression, for a time. [Nares]

insufflation The act of blowing a gas or vapour into a cavity of the body, as when tobacco smoke is injected into the rectum. [Hoblyn] From Latin *sufflatus*, blown up, puffed out. [Stormonth]

interlard To *lard*, or stuff, lean meat with fat. [Bailey] Metaphorically, to mix what is the solid part of a discourse with fulsome and irrelevant matter. Thus we say, "to interlard with oaths, compliments," etc. [Brewer]

invalid's table At Yale college in former times, a table at which those who were not in health could obtain more nutritious food than was supplied at the common board. [Hall]

inwit Conscience, as distinguished from *outwit*, knowledge, ability, information. [Mackay]

isabelle The colour so called is the yellow of soiled calico. . . . It is said that Isabel of Austria, daughter of Philip II, at the siege of Ostend, vowed not to change her linen till the place was taken. As the seige lasted three years [until 1604], we may well suppose that it was somewhat soiled by wear. [Brewer]

J was formerly interchangeable with *i*, the same character being used for both. . . . Even up to a comparatively recent date, *i* and *j* were not separated in English dictionaries, alphabetical lists, &c. As a symbol, *j* is used in medical prescriptions, at the end of a series of numbers for *one*, as *vij*, seven, and *viij*, eight, &c. [R. Hunter]

jack-at-a-pinch A man whose services are used only on an emergency. [Taylor]

jampher A male jilt; an idler; a scoffer. [From] *jamph*, to make a game of; to mock, jeer, sneer; to act the part of a male jilt; to trifle, spend time idly; lounge. [Warrack] SEE *causey-webs*, *slister*

jannocks Fairness; what is fair and proper; "fair jannocks." [Wilkinson]

japers The japers, I apprehend, were the same as the *bourdours*, or *rybauders*, an inferior class of minstrels, and properly called *jesters* in the modern acceptation of the word, whose wit, like the *merry-andrews* of the present day, consisted in low obscenity, accompanied with ludicrous gesticulation. . . . It was a very common and a very favorite amusement, so late as the sixteenth century, to hear the recital of verses and moral speeches, learned for that purpose by a set of men who, without ceremony, intruded themselves not only into taverns and other places of public resort, but also into the houses of the nobility. [Strutt]

jarkman There are some in this Schoole of Beggars that practise writing and reading, and those are called *jarkmen*. Yea, the jarkman is so cunning sometimes that he can speake Latine, which learning of his lifts him up to advancement for by that means he becomes Clarke of their Hall, and his office is to make counterfeit licenses which are called *gybes*, and to which he puts seales, and those are termed *jarkes*. [Dekker] SEE *avering*

jawing-tacks When a person speaks with vociferous fluency, he is said to have "hauled his *jawing-tacks* on board." [Smyth]

jemmie duffs Weepers, so called from a noted Scotsman of the eighteenth century who lived at Edinburgh. His great passion . . . was to follow funerals in mourning costume with orthodox weepers. [Brewer]

jeoparty-trot A quick motion, between running and walking when one, on account of fear or weakness, is not able to run at full speed. [Jamieson]

jimp Dainty, well-formed, well-fitting. [Mackay]

jippo A waistcoat, or kind of stays, for females. [Ogilvie]

jongleur In medieval France, and in England under the Norman kings, a minstrel who went from place to place singing songs, generally of his own composition and generally to his own accompaniment. [Whitney]

jordan A slang name for a chamber utensil. The history of this word is not very clearly made out. It appears as early as 1382. The most probable origin seems to me to be from the name of the river Jordan. Pilgrims on their return from the Holy Land brought back a bottle of water of the sacred river for baptismal purposes, and the bottles themselves seem to have resembled the well-known Florence flask in shape, when emptied, [and] continued to be looked upon as somewhat sacred. Hence, they were employed by chemists for their more delicate operations, and also by certain quack doctors. Owing to the use made of them by the latter, the name came to be applied to any vessel used for a similar purpose. [Phin]

joss To crowd or press together; whence the diminutive *jostle*, to press against in a crowd. [Mackay]

jow-fair A wedding broken off at the last moment, when the contracting parties, or one of them, have arrived at the church; a race broken off at the appointed day. Generally applied to a muddle, or a blundering occurrence. [Taylor]

Judas-hole A small hole cut in a door to enable a person to see into a room without being himself seen. [R. Hunter]

jumart The supposed offspring of a bull and mare, or she-ass; from French *jumart*, a probable corruption of *chimera*, a fabled monster. [Stormonth]

junters A state of sulks. [Robinson, GMY]

jussel A dish made of several sorts of meat minced together; from Latin *jus*, broth. [Ogilvie]

karrows The karrows plaie awaie mantle and all to the bare skin, and then trusse themselves in straw or leaves. They wait for passengers in the highway, invite them to game upon the greene and aske no more but companions to make them sport. For default of other stuffe, they pawne their *glibs* [thick matted locks of hair worn on the forehead], the nailes of their fingers and toes. *Ireland* [Stanyhurst]

keak A distortion or injury of the spine that causes deformity. It seems to have some affinity with the Cheshire word *kench* . . . "a twist or wrench, a strain or sprain." Our term, however, is never used but for a wrench in the spine. [Carr]

kedge-belly In Old English, a glutton who stuffs himself as full as a *keg*; from *kaggi*, a cask fastened as a float to an anchor to show where it is. [Stormonth] SEE *lust-dieted*, *nyaffle*, *pa-pelard*

kelk To groan, belch. *Northern England* [Halliwell]

Kent Street ejectment Taking away the street-door, a method devised by the landlords of Kent Street, Southwark, when their tenants were more than a fortnight in arrears. [Brewer]

key of the street

key of the street A person who has no house to go to at night, or is shut out from his own, is said to have the *key of the street*. [Davies]

kiddliwink A small shop where they retail the commodities of a village store. [Hotten]

kimbly The gift given to the first person who brought news of a birth to those interested; also to the one who brought first news in the smuggling times. [Jago] SEE *piper's news*

king's-weather A name given to the exhalations seen rising from the earth during a warm day. [Jamieson] SEE *queen's weather*

kissingcrust Crust formed where one loaf in the oven touches another. [Johnson] SEE *bread-rasp, tinker's toast*

kiss the cap To put the *cap*, or mug, to the mouth; a phrase for drinking. [Jamieson]

knevel The moustache. The hair on the upper lip was worn for ages before the modern, and now the only, name for the thing was borrowed from the Spanish. The word is now entirely obsolete, but pure English. [Mackay]

knocking-up-stick A long, flexible rod used by the *knocker up*. It has a few buttons attached to its top end, and with these he taps gently at the panes of the bedroom window. [Taylor] SEE *upknocking*

knotchel, cry-notchil When a man publicly declares he will not pay any of his wife's debts contracted since a certain date, she is said to be *knotchelled*; a certain disgraceful imaginary remark. In short, she is a marked woman. [Leigh] In the old time, this was effected by means of the bell-man. It is now done through the medium of newspapers. [Taylor] SEE *piper's news, shachled-shoes*

knoup To toll the church-bell. This observation bore reference to a current belief that when, according to the rites of induction, a clergyman tolls the bells on being put into possession of his church, the number of years he will hold are foretold by the number of strokes on the bell. *Knoup* is evidently a corrupted form of Middle English *knap*, to strike. [Jackson]

knutter A horse is said to knutter in Hampshire when it makes the noise which it does to greet another. So called clearly from the sound. [Holloway]

L is frequently interchanged with *r*, of which it is considered to be a later modification; thus, the Latin *lavendula* has become the English *lavender*. [R. Hunter] SEE *landerer*

laced-mutton A prostitute; a bad woman with fine showy dress, as though a simple sheep were dressed out with lace. [Holloway] In this very common cant expression for a courtesan, the meaning of *laced* has been a good deal disputed. Perhaps the *mutton* has been called *laced* with a quibble—courtesans being notoriously fond of finery, and also frequently subjected to the whip. [Dyce] SEE *dress-lodger*

lagam A term in derelict law for goods which are sunk, with a buoy attached, that they may be recovered. Also, things found on the bottom of the sea. Ponderous articles which sink with the ship in wreck. [From] Anglo-Saxon *liggan*. [Smyth]

lager-wine Old bottled wine; wine which has been kept in the cellar for some time. [Stormonth]

lamb's-wool A favorite liquor among the common people, composed of ale and roasted apples. The pulp of the roasted apple [was] worked up with the ale till the mixture formed a smooth beverage. Fanciful etymologies for this popular word have been thought of, but it was probably named from its smoothness, resembling the wool of lambs. [Nares] Lamb's wool is also a hot drink, well known to the community for centuries. Supposed by some to be derived from *Lammas*, at which time it was drunk. [Hotten]

land-damn To abuse with rancour; *damn* through the *land*. [Huntley] In Old English, to scourge with a dried bull's penis; from Gaelic *lann*, the penis, and *dahm*, an ox. [Stormonth] This word is a Shakespearian puzzle. . . . *Landan*, *lantan* [and] *rantan* are used by some Gloucestershire people in the sense of scouring or correcting to some purpose. [Halliwell] When any slaughterer was detected, or any parties discovered in adultery, it was usual to *landan* them. This was done by the rustics traversing from house to house along the countryside, blowing trumpets or beating drums or kettles. When an audience was assembled, the delinquents' names were thus *land-damned*. *The Winter's Tale* [Dyce]

landerer Originally *launder*, a man employed to wash; whence *laundress*. But query, is this word contracted from French *la-*

vandière, or made from the English word *laund,* a lawn on which clothes were usually dried? [Nares]

landjobber One who buys and sells lands for other men. [Johnson] SEE *stockjobber*

lant Stale urine. It was preserved in a tank, and having been mixed with lime, used for dressing wheat before it was sown to prevent birds from picking up the seeds. [Addy] To *leint* ale, to put urine into it to make it strong. [Ray] Formerly much used by Lancashire cottagers for scouring or cleaning blankets and other woollen cloths; also for sundry medicinal purposes. In every yard or garden would have been found a receptacle for storing it. [Nodal] SEE *chamber-lye*

larks-leers Arable land not in use, much frequented by larks. Any land poor and bare of grass, only fit for larks to build their nests in; [from] *larks' lair.* [Holloway]

latitudinarian One who allows himself great liberties in religious matters. [Walker]

leachcraft The art of medicine or surgery, [from] Saxon *leach, læc,* a physician or surgeon. This word has been used occasionally by very late writers, particularly in the burlesque style, where obsolete words are always retained for a time before they finally perish. [Nares]

lead-water The rain which runs off the lead . . . roof of the church, especially that from the chancel, where the altar is situated, said to be a restorative when sprinkled upon the sick. [Robinson, GYW]

leg-bail Term applied to one who, when charged with any

lead-water

crime or misdemeanor, instead of waiting the course of law, provides for his safety by flight. [Jamieson] Dishonest desertion from duty. The phrase is not confined to its nautical bearing. [Smyth]

lewstery To bustle and stir about, like a lusty wench. [Elworthy] SEE *laced-mutton, rigmutton*

libidinist One who is given to lewdness. [Whitney] SEE *satyriasis*

lick-for-leather One is going *lick-for-leather* when one is at full speed. [Robinson, GMY]

life-arrow An arrow carrying a line or cord, fired from a gun for the purpose of establishing communication between a vessel and the shore in cases of shipwreck. The arrow-head has large barbs, so that it may readily catch in the ship's rigging. [Whitney]

lightning-before-death A proverbial phrase, partly deduced from observation of some extraordinary effort of nature often made in sick persons just before death, and partly from a superstitious notion of an ominous and preternatural mirth supposed to come on at that period, without any ostensible reason. [Nares]

linctus A term applied to soft substances of the consistence of syrup, which are taken by being licked off a spoon. [From] *lingo*, to lick. [Hoblyn]

link-hides Sausage skins, the intestines of a pig, prepared and stuffed. [Forby] SEE *pudding-leather*

lion's-provider A popular but incorrect name for the jackel, and hence applied to anyone who acts as a tool, sycophant or foil to another. [R. Hunter] SEE *toad-eater*

liplabour Action of the lips without concurrence of the mind. Words without sentiment. [Johnson] SEE *mouth-honour*

liripoop A hood of a particular form, formerly worn by graduates. In later times, a scarf or appendage to the hood, consisting of long tails or tippets, which passed round the neck and hung down to the feet, and was often jagged. [Whitney] *Liripoop* and *leripoop* are sometimes used without any definite meaning, chiefly I presume, from their droll and burlesque sound, as . . . Lyly, [who] used it [in *Mother Bombie*, 1594] to express a degree of knowledge or acuteness:

"There's a girl that knows her lerripoop." . . . Probably it meant, at first, having that knowledge which entitled a person to wear a liripoop, or scarf, as a doctor. [Nares]

little snakesman A little boy who gets into a house through the sink-hole, and then opens the door for his accomplices. He is so called from writhing and twisting like a snake, in order to work himself through the narrow passage. [Grose, *DVT*] SEE *figging-law, moon curser, Tyburn-blossom*

liversick Sick at heart. [Grose] Having a diseased liver—that is, in love; from the old notion that the liver is the seat of love. [Whitney]

living tally A man and woman who live together without being married are said to be *living tally*; the man is termed a *tally-husband*, and the woman a *tally-wife*. [Taylor] SEE *handfasting*

liversick

Londonoy A Londoner. *Chaucer* [Halliwell] SEE *Lud's-town*

long-in-the-mouth Tough, requiring a long time to be masticated. [Walker]

lorgeous-days An ejaculation of surprise. Probably a corruption of "Lord Jesus, what days!" [Taylor] SEE *woonkers, yoicks*

lotherwit That you may take amends of him which doth defile your bond-woman [servant] without your license. [Stroud] SEE *childwit*

loup-garou A werewolf, a lycanthrope. [From] French *loup*, a wolf, and *garou*, from Low Latin *gerulphus*, a werewolf. [R. Hunter] SEE *cynanthropy*

love-lock A lock or curl of hair hanging at the ear, worn by men of fashion in the reigns of Elizabeth and James I. [Donald] SEE *repenter curls*

love-tooth A *love-tooth in the head*, an inclination to love. [Nares] SEE *babies-in-the-eyes, sheep's-eye*

lowlyhood Humility. [Mackay]

Lud's-town The ancient name of London . . . rebuilt by [mythical King] Lud. [Phin] SEE *Londonoy*

lust-dieted Feeding gluttonously. [Onions] SEE *nyaffle, papelard*

lustihood Vigour; sprightliness; bodily strength. [Fenning]

lypothymie A fainting or swounding, when the vitall spirits being suddenly opprest, a man sinketh down, as if he were dead. [Bullokar]

maffle To stammer; to stutter. [Mackay]

magsman A street swindler who watches for countrymen and gullible persons, and pursuades them out of their possessions. Magsmen are wonderful actors. Their work is done in broad daylight, without any stage accessories, [when] often a wink, a look, or a slip of the tongue would betray their confederacy. Their ability and perseverance are truly worthy of a better cause. Magsmen are very often men of superior education. Those who work the tidal trains and boats are often faultlessly dressed and highly accomplished. [Hotten]

maiden-rent A [fee] paid by every tenant in the [English] manor of Builth at their marriage; it was anciently given to the lord for his omitting the custom of *marcheta*, whereby . . . he was to have the first night's lodging with his tenant's wife. . . . The custom for the lord to lay the first night with the bride of his tenant was very common in Scotland, and in the north parts of England. But it was abrogated by Malcolme III at the instance of the queen, and instead thereof a mark was paid to the lord by the bridegroom, from whence 'tis called *marcheta muleris*. [Blount, *LD*] SEE *culliage*

majuscule A capital letter, as distinguished from a *minuscule*. Majuscules are found in Latin manuscripts of the sixth century and earlier . . . from *majusculus*, diminutive from *majus*, greater. [R. Hunter]

man-browed Having hair growing between the eyebrows. Here it is deemed unlucky to meet a person thus marked, especially if the first one meets in the morning. Elsewhere, it is a favourable omen. The term, I suppose, had been primarily applied to a woman, as by this exuberance indicating something of a masculine character, having brows like a man. [Jamieson] SEE *blepharon*

man of straw A person without capital. It used to be customary for a number of worthless fellows to loiter about our law-courts to become false witness or surety for anyone who would buy their services. Their badge was a straw in their shoes. [Brewer] To write or speak of a person in trade that he is a *man of straw* is to impute insolvency. [Stroud] SEE *post-knight*

maritagium Strictly taken, the right of the Lord of the Fee to marry the daughters of his vassels after their death. Others tell us it was that profit which might accrue to the lord by the marriage of one under age who held his lands by knight's service. [Blount] SEE *culliage, maiden-rent*

market-peart Exhilarated, rather than positively intoxicated, by drink; a return-from-market condition. [From] *peart*, well in health and bright in spirits. [Jackson]

married all over Said of women who, after their marriages, fall off in their appearance and become poor and miserable-looking.

mastigophorer A fellow worthy to be whipped. [Blount, G] SEE *post-knight*

maulifuff A woman without energy; one who makes much fuss and does little or nothing; generally applied to a young woman. [From] German *mal*, voice, speech, and *pfuffen*, to blow. [Jamieson]

mawmsey Sleepy; stupid, as from want of rest or over-drinking. [Jackson]

maw-wallop A filthy, ill-cooked mess of victuals; [from] *maw*, the stomach. [Mackay]

mazzard A burlesque word for the head, whence *to mazzard*, to knock on the head, to brain one . . . It comes from *mazer*, a bowl. In a similar way, Italian *zucca*, properly a gourd and thence a drinking cup, is used to signify a skull. [Wedgwood]

meatwhole Having a healthy appetite. [Robinson, *DMY*]

mebby-scales To be "in the *mebby-scales*," to waver between two opinions. [Halliwell]

medicinal days The sixth, eighth, tenth, twelfth, sixteenth, eighteenth, etc. of a disease, so called because according to

Hippocrates, no crisis occurs on these days, and medicine may be safely administered. [Brewer] SEE *critical days*

megrim A pain in the head, supposed to arise from the biting of a worm [*vermis capitis*] . . . Hence, as caprices were also supposed to arise from the biting of a maggot, the name megrim was also given to any capricious fancy. The origin of the word [now *migraine*] is Greek *hemi*, half, and *cranium*, skull. [Wedgwood]

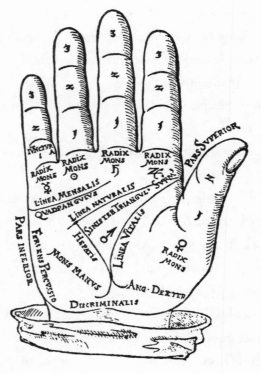

mercurial-finger

melancholia religiosa Melancholy from religious dispair. [J. Coxe]

mercurial-finger The little finger. [R. Hunter] The thumb, in chiromancy, we give to Venus, the forefinger to Jove, the midst to Saturn, the ring to Sol, the least to Mercury. [Jonson] SEE *wedding finger*

meretricious Whorish, such as is practised by prostitutes alluring by false show. [R. Coxe]

merkin Counterfeit hair for women's privy parts. [Grose, *DVT*] SEE *gynacomastax*

merry-go-sorry A mixture of laughing and crying. [R. Hunter] SEE *chantepleur*

metempsychosis The passage of the soul from one body to another; from *meta*, beyond, over, [and] *psyche*, life. [Stormonth]

methomania An irresistible desire for intoxicating substances. [Dunglison]

mex'n To cleanse a stable; to sweep up manure or dirt into a heap, or *mixen*. Used more recently by housewives in the sense of a perfunctory cleaning-up. [Taylor]

midnight friend An acoustic apparatus consisting of a . . . tube extending from the doctor's street door to his bed, by which a message can be transmitted to the awakened practitioner, instead of merely the sound of his bell. Hence, it has been fancifully termed the "medical man's midnight friend." [Hoblyn]

midshipman's-nuts Broken biscuit, eaten by way of [shipboard] dessert. [Farmer]

midwife-gallop Full gallop; a great speed. [Warrack] SEE *egg-wife-trott*

mileway A measure of time [to walk one mile]; the third part of an hour, or twenty minutes. [Whitney] Five of th[e]se degrees maken a milewey, and three milewey maken an howre. [Chaucer, *Astrolabe Treatise*]

milklivered Cowardly, faint-hearted. [Scott]

milkmeat Any food of which milk is an ingredient. [Warrack] A mixture of milk and meat. [Worcester]

milkscore An account of milk owed for, scored on a board. [Johnson] SEE *ale-score*

mimp To make believe; to sham. [Dartnell]

mi-nabs A term used when speaking of a third person who is not present . . . It would appear to be the equivalent of "my lord," or "his lordship," used sarcastically. The word is evidentally derived from the Scottish word *knab* or *nab*, which was used derisively for a little laird, or any person of dignity. [Taylor]

minnie A grandmother. This word, although now in the mouths of the vulgar, is undoubtedly very ancient. It is nearly allied to Belgian *minne*, a wet nurse; *minne-moer*, a nursing mother; *minne-vader*, a foster-father. . . . *To minnie lambs*, to join each lamb belonging to a flock to its own dam, after they have been separated for some time. It is given as proof of the accuracy of a shepherd's acquaintance with his flock, how incredible soever it may seem to those who are strangers to a pastoral life that, after the lambs have been separated from the ewes, he can minnie [each] lamb. [Jamieson]

minnock A favorite darling, or person who is the object of one's affection. [Fenning]

minute-watch A watch in which minutes are more distinctly marked than in common watches, which reckon by the hour. [Johnson]

mirknight Midnight; the darkest hour of night. [Warrack]

miscomfrumple To rumple, crease. If one female sits so close to another as to rumple or crease her dress by pressing or sitting upon it, she is said to *miscomfrumple* it. *Northamptonshire* [J. Wright]

misnancy An effeminate character; one conspicuous for outward adornment and airs of gentility, but deficient in common sense. [Robinson, *DOL*] SEE *puss-gentleman*

missucceed To turn out ill. [Davies]

mistress-piece A chief performance of a woman. Formed on an analogy of *master-piece*. [R. Hunter]

moanworthy Sad. [Halliwell]

mobble To dress grossly or inelegantly. [Walker]

mollynogging Frequenting the company of immoral women. *Lincolnshire* [J. Wright] SEE *mulierosity*

monsterful Wonderful, extraordinary. *Chaucer* [R. Hunter]

month's mind Sometimes defined as monthly commemoration of the dead, but used ludicrously to mean a great or strong desire. Croft explains it as a woman's longing such as sometimes occurs in pregnancy. [Phin] *Month's mind* is a curious instance of a phrase dating from before the Reformation, surviving in common speech long after its original meaning has been forgotten. The month's mind were masses said at a month after the death of a deceased person, for the repose of his soul, the word *mind* meaning memorial, or remembrance. . . . There were also *year's*, and *two years' mind* observed. [Long]

moon-blink A temporary evening blindness occasioned by sleeping in the moonshine in tropical climates; it is technically designated *nyctalopia*. [Smyth]

moon curser A *link-boy*, or one that, under [pretense of guiding] men, robs them or leads them to a gang of rogues that will do it for them. [Smith] SEE *figging-law, little snakesman, Tyburn-blossom*

moon-dial A dial marking the time by moonlight. [Zell]

morganatic A *morganatic marriage* is one between a man of superior and a woman of inferior rank, in which it is stipulated that the latter and her children shall not enjoy the rank, nor inherit the possessions of her husband. [Brande] In these marriages, the husband gives his left hand to the bride instead of the right when he says, "I take thee for my wedded wife." [Brewer]

mort-head A large turnip excavated with the representation of a face cut through the side, and a lighted candle put within. This is carried about [at] night by mischievious boys as an object of terror. [Jamieson]

mort-safe A frame of cast iron with which a coffin is surrounded during five or six weeks for the purpose of preventing the robbery of the grave. [Jamieson]

motch To eat little, slowly, quietly and secretly; to consume or waste imperceptibly. Hence, *motching*, fond of dainties, with the idea of eating in secret. [Also] slow, quiet eating, with the idea of fondness for good living; imperceptible use, with the notion of thriftlessness. *Banffshire* [J. Wright] SEE *chimble*

mountain of pity A stock of money raised by charity of good people who, observing the poor ruined by usury . . . voluntarily contributed good store of treasure to be preserved and lent to them, whereby they might have money at a low rate to relieve their wants. [Blount, G]

mouse-web A cobweb; phlem in the throat. [Warrack]

mouth-honour Civility outwardly expressed, without sincerity. [R. Coxe] SEE *liplabour*

mucksluff An overcoat put on to cover the defects of one's underclothing. *Yorkshire* [J. Wright] SEE *cover-slut*

mulberry mania The craze during the 1830s for planting mulberry trees in expectation of making profits in the silk industry. [Mathews] SEE *tulipomania*

mulierosity [From] *mulierose*, too much addicted to the love of women. [Bailey] Unlawful lust after properly married or defiled women; for *mulier* signifies a woman that hath the company of a man. [Blount, G] SEE *mollynogging*

mulligrubs A pretended or counterfeit sullenness; a resolute, fixed and artificial displeasure, in order to gain some point desired. [Dyche] A twisting of the guts, so called from the symptomatic fever attending it; from British *mugl* or *mul*, warm. A low word. [Fenning] *Grub* was once the usual word for a worm, and in Latin the same discomfort is *verminatio*, from *vermis*, a worm. [Grose, *DVT*]

mundivagant Wandering through the world. [Blount, G] SEE *vagation*

murlimews Blessings and crossings which the papisticall priests doe use in their holy water to make a *mearlew muse*. [Hollyband]

music-duffer Among the swag-shopkeepers, at one place in Houndsditch more especially, are dealers in "duffing-fiddles." These are German-made instruments, and are sold to the street-folk at two shillings, sixpence, or three shillings, bow and all. Then purchased by the music-duffers, they are discoloured so as to be made to look old. A music-duffer, assuming the way of a man half-drunk, will enter a public-house, or accost any party in the street, saying, "It cost me two guineas and another fiddle . . . but I may as well be my own broker, for I must have money anyhow, and I'll sell it for ten shillings." [Mayhew] SEE *widow's piano*

myomancy A kind of divination by means of mice. [Stormonth]

nab-nanny A louse; [from] *nab*, to catch, and *nanny*, the nursemaid, whose business it was to catch them. *Norfolk, Suffolk* [Holloway]

nacks A disease to which fowls are subject, in consequence of having taken too much hot food, such as warm porridge. It causes severe wheezing and breathlessness, resembling the croup in children. . . . The vulgar cure in Lothian is to smear the nostrils with butter and snuff. [Jamieson] SEE *bait-pot*

naked-bed A person undressed in his bed was formerly said to be *in naked-bed* and, according to Brockett, the phrase is still in use applied to anyone entirely naked. The term was probably derived from the ancient custom of sleeping without night linen, which was most common in this country during the thirteenth, fourteenth and fifteenth centuries. [Halliwell]

Napier's bones Small rods, arranged by Lord Napier to expedite arithmetical calculations. [Smyth] SEE *numbering machine*

natkin A disagreeable taste or smell. [Warrack] SEE *carfumish, feff, odor of sanctity*

nattlesome Short-tempered; quarrelsome. [Taylor] SEE *fratchy*

naufrage When, by the violent agitation of the waves, the impetuosity of the winds, the storm, or the lightning, a vessel is swallowed up or so shattered that there remain only the pieces, the accident is called *naufrage*. [Bouvier] SEE *vorago*

nazzle A child who has been guilty of deceptive practices is termed a "little nazzle." Never applied to the male sex. [Robinson, *DOL*]

neck-verse The verse read by a malefactor, to entitle him to *benefit of clergy* [originally a pardon for Latin-savvy priests], and therefore eventually to save his life. Generally, the first verse of the 51st Psalm. [Nares]

neeze To go in search of birds' nests; [from] *neeze*, a nest. [Taylor] SEE *cragsman*

negrofy To turn into a negro. [Davies]

nerled Ill-treated, as by a step-mother; [from] Belgian *knarren*, to snarl. [Holloway]

nestcock One that never was [away] from home; a fondling or wanton. [Blount, G] *Nest-cockle*, the last-hatched bird in a neast. [Cotgrave] SEE *burdalone*

nicknackitarian A dealer in curiosities, such as Egyptian mummies, Indian implements of war, arrows dipped in the poison of the upas-tree, bows, antique shields, helmets, &c. [Hone]

nightfoundered Distressed for want of knowing the way in the night. [Barclay]

nighttripping Going lightly in the night. [Johnson]

ninny-broth Popular name for coffee. [Nares] SEE *chatter-broth, purl, saloop*

nizzertit Stunted in growth. [Warrack] SEE *nurgling*

Noah's ark A cloud appearing when the sky is, for the most part, clear, much resembling a large boat turned bottom up-wards, considered a sure prognostic of rain. *Norfolk* [Holloway] If it extends south to north, it is viewed as an indication of good weather; if from east to west, a squall of wind or rain is certainly looked for. [Jamieson] Noah's ark, which being occasioned by a brisk west-wind rolling together a large number of bright clouds into the form of a ship's hull . . . is pointed north and south, and said to be an infallible sign of rain to happen within twenty-four hours. [Clarke] SEE *devil's smiles, stelliscript, thwankin*

nobbler A small drink of spirits, wine or beer. Whence, to *nobblerise*. [Baker] A glass of spirits; literally that which *nobbles*, or gets hold of you. *Nobble* is the frequentative form of *nab*. No doubt there is an allusion to the bad spirits frequently sold at bush public-houses, but if a teetotaler had invented the word, he could not have invented one involving stronger condemnation. [Morris]

noctuary An account of what passes in the night; the converse of a diary. [Annandale]

noggle To walk awkwardly. [Mackay] SEE *cramble*

nonnaturals Anything which is not naturally, but by accident or abuse, the cause of disease. Physicians reckon these to be six: air, diet, sleep, exercise, excretion, and the passions. [Walker]

nooningscaup The labourer's resting time after dinner. The word is formed from *nooning*, noon, and *scope*, used for liberty or privilege. The termination *ing* is generally put to *noon*, as well as to *morn* and *even*. [Watson]

nose-bag A visitor to a house of refreshment who brings his own victuals and calls for a glass of water or lemonade. The reference is to carrying the feed of a horse in a nose-bag to save expense. [Brewer]

nowl The head of an animal, as distinguished from that of a man. [Mackay]

nude contract Without consideration given, where no action can arise. [Coles]

numbles, umbles Praecordia, as the hart, the spleene, the lunges, and liver. [Elyot] To "eat [h]umble pie," to eat one's own words; to be obliged to act in a very humiliating way— that is, to stoop, as it were, to eat a pie made of *umbles*. [Stormonth]

nurgling A person of a *nurring* [active, clever], or cat-like dis-

nude contract

position; [related to] *nurgle*, also *nurg*, a short, squat, little savage man. [Mactaggart] SEE *nizzertit*

nurk The worst pig of the litter. [Dartnell]

nyaffle To eat in a hasty, gluttonous manner. [Batchelor] SEE *crapulous, lust-dieted, puzzomous, soft-wind*

nympholepsy A frenzy occasioned by seeing one of the nymphs; from Greek *lambano*, I take. [Stormonth]

oblat A soldier who, grown impotent or maimed in service, hath maintenance or the benefit of a monk's place assigned him in an abbey. [Blount, G]

odor of sanctity The Catholics tell us that good persons die in the *odour of sanctity*, and there is a certain truth in the phrase, for when one honoured by the Church dies, it is not unusual to perfume the room with incense and sometimes embalm the body. . . . The Catholic notion that priests bear about with them an odour of sanctity may be explained in a similar manner. They are so constantly present when the censers diffuse sweet odour that their clothes and skin smell of the incense. [Brewer] SEE *carfumish, feff, natkin, second-scent*

off-capped Took off their caps, in the usual form of courtesy. *Othello* [Phin] SEE *borrower's cap, hat-worship*

off-capped

offmagandy The best and choicest of delicacies. Rich, stiff cream would be described as "real offmagandy." [Darlington] SEE *pulpatoon*

ogerhunch Any frightful or loathsome creature, especially a bat. [Edmondston]

oil of angels A gift or bribe of money, the reference being of course to the coin, the "angel." [Davies] SEE *raddlings*

old-man When miners have got into some old works, of which they had previously no knowledge, they say they have *got into an old-man, or t'old man's been there.* [Carr]

olfact To smell much or often. [Coles]

omnium Aggregate of certain portions of different stocks in the public funds. [Browne]

opera-glass A kind of glass constructed in a small wooden tube, so as to view a person in a theater, and, as the glass is made to point at a different object from that which is viewed, it may be used without any one knowing exactly who is observed. [Crabb]

ornithoscopy Watching birds for the purpose of divination. [Davies]

orotund Elocution. Noting a manner of uttering the elements of speech which exhibits them with a fullness, clearness, strength and smoothness, and a ringing or musical quality rarely heard in ordinary speech. [From] Latin *os, oris*, the mouth, and *rotundus*, round. [Worcester]

ostentiferous That which brings monsters or strange sights. [Blount, G]

othergates Otherways; in another manner. The word *gate* here is an Old English and Scotch word which signifies *way* or *road*. *Northern England* [Phin]

outcumlins Strangers, coming from without; not dwelling in the neighbourhood. [Holloway] SEE *cockwalk, foot-ale, gutterblood*

outfangtheefe That theeves or felons . . . out of your land or fee, taken with felony or stealing, shall be brought back to your court and there judged. [Rastell]

out-mouth A full, sensuous mouth. [Whitney]

outparamour To exceed in keeping paramours or mistresses. *King Lear* [Worcester]

out-woman To excell as a woman. [Davies]

over-empty To make too empty. [Johnson]

oxgang Oxgang, as a land measure, was no certain quantity, but as much as an ox could *gang over*, or cultivate. Also called a *bovate*. The Latin *jugum* was a similar term. . . . Eight ox-gangs made a *curucate*. [Brewer] Commonly taken for fifteen acres. [Worcester]

oxter-lift As much as can be carried between the arm and the side, or in a semicircle formed by the arms and the breast. [From] *oxter*, the armpit, the breast. [Warrack]

oyster part An actor who appears, speaks or acts only once. Like an oyster, he opens but once. [Brewer]

pack and penny day The last day of a fair, when bargains are usually sold. [Jennings]

packpaunch A devourer. [Davies] SEE *kedge-belly, lust-dieted*

palliard A vagabond who slept on the straw in barns. From French *paille*, straw. Hence, a dissolute rascal, a lecher, a debauchee. [Shipley] He that goeth in a patched cloke, and hys *doxy* [female companion] goeth in like apparrell. [Awdeley] SEE *gyrovagues, sorn*

pannade The curvettings, prancings or boundings of lustie horses. [Cotgrave]

pantler The servant in a great household whose business it is to attend to the bread [French *pain*], as it is that of a *butler* to attend to the wine. [Mackay]

papelard A flatterer; a hypocrite; from Italian *pappalardo*, a glutton. [Whitney] SEE *greasy tongue, puzzomous, soft-wind*

papmeat Milk for babies. [Davies] SEE *milkmeat*

parentate To celebrate one's parents' funerals. [Cockeram]

parish-garden A vulgarism for *Paris-garden;* [according to] Blount's *Glossographia,* "The place on the Thames bankside at London where the bears are kept and baited. It was anciently so called from Robert de Paris, who had a house and garden there in Richard II's time." [Phin]

parish-top A top bought for public exercise in a parish . . . on which Mr. Steevens says, "This is one of the customs now laid aside: A large top was formerly kept in every village, to be whipped in frosty weather, that the peasants might be kept warm by exercise, and out of mischief while they could not work." [Nares]

parliament-heel The situation of a ship, when she is made to stoop a little to one side [or *careen*], so as to clean the upper part of her bottom on the other side, and cover it with a new composition, and afterwards to perform the same office on that part of the bottom which was first immersed. The application of a new composition, or coat of stuff, on this occasion, is called *boot-topping.* [Falconer]

parnel A priest's mistress. [Shipley] A punk, a slut; the diminutive of [Italian] *petronalla.* [Johnson] SEE *cradle crown, mollynogging*

party-jury A jury in some trials, half foreigners and half natives. [Johnson]

pastorauling Playing at "shepherds and shepherdesses"; used of lovers walking in the fields together. [Warrack]

peascod wooing If a young woman, while she is shelling peas, meets with a pod of nine [peas], the first young man who crosses the threshold afterwards is to be her husband. [Hazlitt] SEE *codders*

peccable Liable to sin . . . from Italian *pecco* [Latin *peccare*], to sin. [Donald]

peddlers' way A road laid down in old maps of Norfolk, by which peddlers formerly travelled. The same, probably, as a *pack-way* . . . a bridle-road, on which pack-horses could travel, but not carriages. [Holloway]

pedlar's French The cant language, used by vagabonds, thieves, &c. [Nares]

peg-tankard A drinking vessel in which a peg or knob is inserted to mark the level to which one person's draught is allowed to lower the liquor. These tankards are said to have contained two quarts, and to have been divided by pegs into eight equal draughts. [Whitney] Our Saxon ancestors were accustomed to use peg-tankards . . . [so] that when two or more drank from the same bowl, no one might exceed his fair proportion. We are told that St. Dunstan introduced the fashion to prevent brawling. [Brewer] SEE *pitch-tankard, pottle-draught*

pelf [From] Old French *pelfre*, goods, especially such as are taken by force, plunder. [Wedgwood] Rubbish; whence pelf, the philosophic term for money, often applied by cynics, who by no means think money the rubbish they assert. The metaphorical use of the word has entirely superseded the original. Ill-gotten gains are called *pelfry*. [Mackay]

penitentiary highball A mixture of strained shellac and milk. The shellac is run through cheesecloth or through the pithy part of a loaf of bread; the denatured alcohol is thus almost freed of gums and resins. Milk is added as an antidote. [Goldin]

penny-wisdom Wisdom or prudence in small matters, used with reference to the phrase, *penny-wise and pound-foolish*, and implying foolishness. [Whitney] SEE *camel-swallower*

peppering shower One in which the rain descends like hail, or like the pepper from the peppering-box. [Watson] SEE *by planets, falling-weather*

peter-grievous Children who look as if they thought themselves sadly put upon by their elders are said to be *peter-grievous*. [Dartnell] From French *petit grief*. [Long]

pettilashery Petty larceny. [Judges]

pewfellow One who sits in the same pew; hence a companion. [Whitney]

pharmacopolist One who sells medicines. [Webster]

phlegmagogue A purge of a milder sort, supposed to evacuate phlegm and leave other humours. [Walker]

phrenology A doctrine which professes to found a philosophy of the human mind upon a presumed knowledge of the functions of different portions of the brain, obtained by comparing their relative forms . . . in individuals with the

pharmacopolist

propensities and intellectual powers which these individuals . . . possess. [Annandale] SEE *amativeness*

phylactery A bandage on which was inscribed some memorable sentence. [Browne]

physick's lye tea Hickory ashes, one quart; soot, half a pint; boiling water. Mix, and allow to stand for twenty-four hours, then decant. An excellent antacid medicine. [Hoblyn]

picktooth Leisurely, as it is in leisure moments that the toothpick is usually employed. [Davies]

pig-puzzle A gate fixed to swing both ways to meet a post. [J.

Wright] So that an animal pushing it from either side cannot get through. [Lowsley]

pigsnye [From] Anglo-Saxon *piga*, a virgin. [Worcester] A darling, a pet, a "dear little eye," commonly used as an endearing form of address to a girl. [Skeat] The Romans used *oculus*, the eye, as a term of endearment, and perhaps *piggesnie*, in vulgar language . . . the eyes of a pig being remarkably small. [Tyrwhitt] SEE *bellibone, cowfyne, snoutfair*

pig's whisper A loud whisper, one meant to be heard. [Patterson]

pilgarlick One who peels garlick for others to eat, who is made to endure hardships or ill-usage while others are enjoying themselves at his expense. [Wedgwood] Said originally to mean one whose skin or hair had fallen off from some disease, chiefly a venereal one, but now commonly used by persons speaking of themselves, as, "There stood poor *pilgarlick*," there stood I. [Grose, *DVT*]

piper's news News that everyone has already heard; probably from a piper going from place to place and still relating the same story, till it be in everyone's mouth. [Jamieson]

pismire The old name of the ant, an insect very generally named from the sharp urinous smell of an ant-hill. [From] Dutch *miere, pismiere*, an ant. [Wedgwood]

pissupprest The suppression of a horse's urine. [Coles]

pitcherings When any young men meet with an acquaintance [who is] in company with his sweetheart, they put in their claim for "pitcherings," or for a sum of money to be given by the male, which is spent in ale, and the courtship is ever afterwards duly recognised. Should he be discovered again with a fresh companion, the claim is renewed. [Robinson, *DOL*]

pitch-tankard A tankard covered inside with pitch. The pitch gives a flavour and perhaps a medicinal value to the beverage which the tankard contains. Pitch-tankards are still used in Germany with certain kinds of beer, such as Lichtenhainer. The modern German pitch-tankards are made of wooden staves held together by wooden hoops, and the ancient English pitch-tankards were made in the same way. [Whitney] SEE *peg-tankard*

pittancer The officer in a monastery who distributed the *pittance*, an allowance or dole of food and drink. [Whitney]

pixilated Led astray, as if by pixies; confused, bewildered, intoxicated. [Mathews] SEE *blutterbunged*

pizzle-grease A popular ointment made of lard boiled from a hog's pizzle. *Alabama, Georgia* [Wentworth]

placeparted Sent out of the world in peace. [Webster] SEE *sleepaway*

planet-ruler An astrologer; a person who professed to tell fortunes by the aid of the stars. [Taylor] SEE *stelliscript, weatherspy*

plumpendicular Perpendicular [to the ground]. By no means a bad word, deriving it from *plumb*, plumb-line, and *pendeo*, Latin to hang; that is, to hang perpendicularly, as a line does with a piece of lead at the end of it. [Holloway]

podware A name given to beans, peas, tares, vetches, and such vegetables as have pods. *Kent* [J. Wright] SEE *chinees, codders, peascod wooing*

poeteeze To write poetry. [Warrack] SEE *rhyming-ware*

pogonophobia A fear of beards. [T. Wright]

pointing-stock Something made the object of ridicule. [Walker] SEE *talkingstock*

poosk To search for vermin on the person. *Shetland Islands* [Jamieson] SEE *pulicosity*

pope's-eye A peculiar little part in a leg of mutton, much esteemed by lovers of that joint. [Hotten] The gland in the middle of the thigh with fat, perhaps so called from its being as tender as the eye. [Fenning] SEE *colonial goose*

pornocracy The rule of prostitutes; dominating influence of courtezans. [From] *The Pornocracy*, a party which controlled the government of Rome and elections to the papacy throughout the first part of the tenth century. [Whitney]

posset A particular sort of liquor made by mixing milk with beer or wine . . . which, occasioning the milk to curdle and the curd being skimmed off, the remaining liquor is called . . . *posset*. [Dyche] A drink composed of hot milk, curdled by some strong infusion, which was much in favour with our ancestors, both as luxury and medicine. [Nares]

postillion One who rides on the first pair of six horses belonging to a coach in order to guide them. [Fenning]

post-knight A knight of the post, a notorious perjurer . . . one who gets his living by giving false evidence. [Skeat] Persons who haunted the purlieus of the courts, ready to be hired for a bribe to swear anything, so called from their being always found waiting at the *posts* which the sheriffs set up outside their doors for posting proclamations on. [Brewer] SEE *man of straw, mastigophorer*

potsheen-twang A lie; the power of lying. A "double potsheen twang," a hell of a lie. [From] *potsheen, poteen,* whisky, especially that which has been distilled illegally. *Ireland* [J. Wright]

pottle-draught The drinking of a *pottle* [a four-pint tankard] of liquor at a draught. [Zell] SEE *peg-tankard, thurindale, woolsorter*]

potvaliant Heated with courage from strong drink. [Johnson]

powfag To tire bodily from overwork; to become worn out in mind from care or anxiety; to work to the point of exhaustion. [Taylor]

preaching-cross A cross erected in the highway, at which monks and others were wont to preach to the public. [Ogilvie]

Preadamite A denomination given to the inhabitants of the earth, conceived by some people to have lived before Adam. [Buck]

pretended pregnancy The criminal act of a female who, not having been delivered, presents an infant as having been born of her. This term . . . likewise includes the case of a female who, having been delivered of a dead child, substitutes for it a living child which is not hers. [Dunglison]

preternuptual A *preternuptual person* is a delicate expression for an adulterer. [Davies] SEE *bedswerver, spouse-breach*

primovant In ancient astronomy, that sphere which was supposed to carry the fixed stars in their daily motions, to which all the other orbs were attached. [Whitney] SEE *extramundane, firmament, stelliscript*

prinkle The flesh is said to *prinkle* when there is a tingling sensation, consequent upon a temporary suspension of the circulation. [Mackay]

probang A long, slender rod of whalebone, with a piece of sponge at its extremity, intended to push down extraneous bodies, arrested in the oesophagus, into the stomach. [Dunglison]

prorump To break forth; burst out. [Whitney]

prunk Proud, vain, saucy. [J. Wright]

prygman A prygman goeth with a stycke in hys hand like an idle person. His propertye is to steale cloathes of[f] the hedge, which they call *storing of the rogeman*, or else filtch poultry, carying them to the alehouse, which they call the *bowsyng in[n]*, and ther syt playing at cardes and dice tyl that is spent which they have so fylched. [Awdeley]

pseudologer A false teacher, a liar. [Blount, G]

psychoblast The germ from which a soul is developed. [Whitney]

psychomachy A conflict of the body with the soul. [Walker]

psychopannuchist One who believed that the soul, after death, entered on an eternal night or sleep. [Davies]

pudding-leather The stomach. *Banffshire* [J. Wright] SEE *link-hides*

puddingtime The time of dinner; the time at which pudding, anciently the first dish, is set upon the table. [Johnson] A person who arrives in time for dinner is said to be "in puddin'-time." Boiled suet puddings used to be the first course of a farmhouse or school dinner. [Taylor]

pugil What is taken up between the thumb and two first fingers. [Browne] SEE *fingerfull, yeepsen*

puke-stocking "Wilt thou rob this . . . *puke-stocking* [knave]?" *1 Henry IV*. Here, puke-stocking probably means dark-coloured, perhaps equivalent to *puce*. That it describes the material of the stocking or hose is less likely. [Dyce]

pulicosity An abundance of, or being full of, fleas. [Fenning] SEE *poosk*

pullikins *Pelican* is the name of a dentist's forceps. Naturally, *pullikin* resulted and the "*s*" was added, on the analogy of *tongs, pincers*, etc. [Wentworth] SEE *gryphus*

pulpatoon A dish made of rabbits, fowl, etc., in a crust of forced [stuffed] meat. [Skeat] A particular sort of confection or cake . . . probably made of *pulp* of fruit, as apple-paste, &c. [Nares] SEE *offmagandy*

pulpitarian A preacher. [Davies]

purl A beverage formed by the infusion of *absinthium*, or common wormwood, in ale. [Hoblyn] A favorite morning drink to produce an appetite, sometimes with gin and spice added. [Hotten] There is yet another class of itinerant dealers . . .

þulpatoon

the river beer-sellers, or *purlmen* as they are more commonly called. [Mayhew]

purseproud Haughty on account of wealth. [Fenning]

puss-gentleman An effeminate dandy. [Whitney] SEE *misnancy*

pussyvan A flurry, temper. Also in the form *pussivent*. [Dartnell]

putage Fornication on the woman's part. [Coles]

putter-out One who deposited money with a party on going abroad, on condition of receiving a great interest for it on his return, proportionable to the dangers of the journey and the chances of his arrival to claim it. [Halliwell]

puttingstone In Scotland, the name of a stone laid at the gates of great houses for trials of strength. [Browne]

puzzomous Disgustingly obsequious. [Robinson, *GWW*]

quackle To interrupt breathing, to choke; from the noise uttered by a person in the act of being choked. *Norfolk, Suffolk, Cambridgeshire* [Holloway]

quadrigamist A man four times married. [Blount, G]

quafftide Time of drinking. [Davies]

quanked Overpowered by fatigue. [Dartnell]

queachy Shaking, quivering; [from] *queach*, a bog, a morass. [Mackay]

queen's tobacco-pipe A peculiarly shaped kiln belonging to the Customs, and situated near the London docks, in which are collected damaged tobacco and cigars, and contraband goods, as tobacco, cigars, tea, &c., which have been smuggled, till a sufficient quantity has been accumulated, when the whole is set fire to and consumed. [R. Hunter]

queen's weather A fine day for a fête, so called because Queen Victoria is, for the most part, fortunate in having fine weather when she appears in public. [Brewer] SEE *king's-weather*

queer-gotten Used of uncertain parentage. [Warrack] SEE *gutterblood, side-slip, town-husband*

queer plungers Cheats who throw themselves into the water, in order that they may be taken up by their accomplices, who carry them to one of the houses appointed by the Humane Society for the recovery of drowned persons, where they are rewarded by the society with a guinea each; and the supposed drowned person, pretending he was driven to that extremity by great necessity, is also frequently sent away with a contribution in his pocket. [Grose, *DVT*]

quiddanet A sweete mixture, thicker than sirupe, and not so thicke nor stiffe as marmalet. [Bullokar]

quidnunc An inquisitive person, always seeking for news. The [Latin] words translated simply signify, "What now?" [Hotten] SEE *kimbly, piper's news*

quigger In the phrase, *as near as a quigger,* as near as may be. [Evans]

quignogs Ridiculous notions or conceits. *Cornwall* [J. Wright]

quire bird A quire bird is one that came lately out of prison, and goeth to seek service. He is commonly a seeker of horses, which they term a *prigger of palfreys*. [Awdeley]

quockerwodger A wooden toy figure which, when pulled by a string, jerks its limbs about. The term is used in a slang sense to signify a pseudo-politician, one whose strings are pulled by somebody else. [Hotten]

quodlibetarian One who talks or disputes on any subject; [from] *quodlibet*, a nice point; a subtilty. [Johnson] SEE *sea-lawyer*

quop To throb with pain. *Midlands* [J. Wright]

quother To talk in a low and confidential tone. [Robinson, GWW]

rabbit's-kiss A penalty in the game of "forfeits" in which a man and a woman have each to nibble the same piece of straw until their lips meet. [Warrack] SEE *cataglottism, deosculation*

rabble-fish A fisherman recognises two general classes of fish, such as are saleable in the market and such as are not so. The latter is termed *rabble-fish* . . . perfectly wholesome, and therefore the food of the fisherman and his family, but yet not sufficiently esteemed to be sold in the market. *Cornwall* [J. Wright]

rack of the eye To determine by the *rack of the eye* is to be guided solely by the eye, without line or rule. [Walker]

rack-rent Rent raised to the uttermost. [Johnson] Rent of, or approaching to, the full annual value of the property out of which it issues. [Stroud]

raddlings Money employed in bribing at elections. [T. Wright] SEE *oil of angels*

ragrowtering Playing at romps, and thereby rumpling, roughening and tearing the clothes to rags, or playing the rogue in a wanton frolic; from *ragery* and *rout,* tumultus. [Elworthy] Playing at romps, which makes *rags grow;* [from] *rag-growth.* [Holloway]

ramfeezled To exhaust oneself with work, to wear oneself out;

ratt-rime

used only in past participle. *Scotland* [J. Wright] SEE *for-swunk*

ratherest Most of all. In use from 1420 to Elizabethan times. [Onions]

rattle-bladder A bladder filled with [dried] peas or the like to make a noise, used in frightening birds off corn. [Davies]

ratt-rime Originally, a rhyme or piece of poetry used in charming and killing rats. The term . . . came to mean halting metres, doggerel, a tirade of nonsense. [Jamieson] The fanciful idea that rats were commonly rhymed to death in Ireland arose probably from some metrical charm or incantation used there for that purpose. [Nares] SEE *rhyming-ware*

raw-gabbit Speaking confidently on a subject of which one is ignorant. [Warrack]

ready-comb In farm houses in this district, a comb was hung by a string to the kitchen door, by which the men-servants combed their hair. White, in his *Antiques of Selborne*, says: "The author remembers to have seen in great farm houses a family comb chained to a post, for the use of the hinds [servants] when they came in to their meals." [Addy]

redder's lick The stroke which one often receives in endeavouring to part combatants. [Jamieson]

red-lattice phrases It is said that a lattice window painted red was formerly a common distinction of an alehouse; hence, *red-lattice phrases*, alehouse talk. [Phin]

redubbers *Redubbours* are those that buy cloth, which they know to be stoln, and turn it into some other form or fashion. [Blount, G] Patchers, botchers, menders of apparel. [From Old Norman] *redubbours de bras*. [Bouvier]

regrator He that hath corn, victuals or other things sufficient for his owne necessary need, occupation or spending, and doth nevertheless ingrosse and buy up into his hands more corn, victuals, or other such things, to the intent to sell the same againe at a higher and deerer price in faires, markets and other such like places. [Rastell] Said to be derived from French *regratter*, to scrape over again, from frauds practised in the dressing or scraping of secondhand cloth to sell again. [Brande]

rejumble Of food, to ferment; to rise in the stomach. The workings of the stomach. *Lincolnshire* [J. Wright]

remittance-man One who derives the means of an inglorious and frequently dissolute existence from the periodical receipt of money from Europe. [Morris]

renterfuge A rendezvous, especially a place haunted by birds. Probably a corruption of *rendezvous*. *Suffolk* [J. Wright] SEE *chyrme*

repenter curls The long ringlets of a lady's hair. *Repentir* is the French for a penitentiary, and *les repenties* are the girls sent there for reformation. . . . Mary Magdelane is represented to have had such long hair that she wiped off her tears from the feet of Jesus. Hence, *Magdalen curls* would mean the long hair of a Mary Magdalen made into ringlets. [Brewer] SEE *love-lock*

repurple To make purple again, to doubly dye with purple. [Davies]

rere-banket A second course of sweets or desserts after dinner; probably for *rear-* (that is, *after*) *banquet* . . . A *rere-supper* seems to have been a late or second supper. [Nares] SEE *eattocks*

restial A fee for burial within the Church, including the charge for tolling the bell. [Jackson] SEE *ground-mail*

resurrectionist A body-snatcher. [Farmer] As soon as the body was raised, it was generally placed in a sack, and then carried to a hackney-coach or spring-cart. When bodies were sent from the country to the metropolis, they were . . . generally

resurrectionist

deposited in some half-built house, or other convenient building, until the following day. The body-snatcher would then, dressed as a porter, swing the load over his shoulders, and often, even in broad daylight, carry it to its place of destination through the most crowded streets of the metropolis. [R. Chambers]

retrocopulation A joyning or coupling backward. [Blount, G]

rhonchisonant Imitating the noise of snorting. [Coles] SEE *roxle*

rhyming-ware Composition in rhyme; poetry. *Scotland* [Jamieson] SEE *poeteeze, trencher-poetry*

ribroast To beat soundly. [Fenning]

ride-and-tie When two people agree to ride a horse in turn, the method of travelling is called *ride-and-tie*. When one has ridden the horse for some distance, he ties him to a gate, &c., and walking on, leaves his comrade to ride the horse and overtake him. [Addy] SEE *shanks'-pony*

right croaker A physician who does business with the underworld, treating wounds without reporting to police. [Goldin]

rigmutton A wanton wench that is ready to ride upon men's backs, or else passively to be their rompstall. The word *mutton*, when applied to a woman, whether alone or part of a compound epithet, seems always to have been opprobrious; *rigmutton-rumpstall*, a wanton girl. . . . [From] *rig, rigging*, ready to bestride any inactive stallion, and give him a quickening spur. [Elworthy] SEE *laced-mutton*

road-proud Crops which look well from the road, but are not so good as they look, are said to be *road-proud*. [Parish] SEE *runaway-crop*

road steamer A locomotive adapted to run on common roads. [Annandale]

rooped Hoarse, as with bronchitis. [Mackay] SEE *thorough cough*

root-house A house made of roots. [R. Hunter]

roozles Wretchedness of mind; the "miserables." *Midlands* [Northall]

rostral-crown The naval crown [medal] anciently awarded to the individual who first boarded an enemy's ship. [Smyth]

rough and ugly Well in health. *Norfolk, Suffolk* [J. Wright]

round and square Everywhere. [Halliwell]

rounstow To cut off the ears of sheep, and so obliterate distinctive marks of ownership. [Warrack] He flung his marches open to his neighbour's sheep, and when they came upon his land, he *rounstow'd* their ears. [Mactaggart] SEE *clicking-fork't, shepherd's book*

rowel To insert a circular piece of leather, with a hole in the centre, into a wound to cause a discharge of humours. [Skeat]

roxle To grunt. [Mackay] SEE *rhonchisonant*

ruckle A loose heap or pile; figuratively, a *ruckle of bones*, a very lean person. *Yorkshire* [J. Wright] SEE *shail-about*

rudderish Hasty, passionate. *Southwest England* [J. Wright] SEE *ferry-whisk, fluckadrift, shirty*

rudesby A rude person. [Nares] . . . *-by* [is] a termination found also in *idlesby*, *sneaksby*, and *suresby*, by some taken to be a reduced form of *boy*. [Whitney]

rue-bargain, rue-penny A man repents of his purchase, and offers the seller so much to take it back again, which is said to be the "rue-bargain." [Robinson, *GYW*] When a man withdraws his banns of marriage, he considers it a *rue-bargain*. [Halliwell]

ruffler The ruffeler goeth wyth a weapon to seeke service, saying he hath bene a servitor in the wars, and beggeth for his reliefe. But his chiefest trade is to rob poor wayfaring men and market women. [Awdeley]

ruly Obedient; as good and necessary a word as *unruly*, which remains in the language. [Mackay]

rumbustical [From] French *rabaster*, to make a clatter or disturbance. [Cotgrave] Boisterous, overbearing. [T. Wright]

runaway-crop Thin or bad crop of corn or turnips on the Isle of Wight. [Halliwell] SEE *road-proud*

runcy A woman of coarse manners and doubtful character. *Banffshire* [J. Wright] SEE *rigmutton*

runnet A liquor made by steeping the stomach of a calf in hot water, and used in curdling milk. Sometimes, but improperly, spelt *rennet*. [Fenning]

running stationer A hawker of books, ballads, dying speeches, and newspapers. Persons of this class formerly used to run with newspapers, blowing a horn, when they were sometimes termed *flying stationers*. Nowadays, in the event of any political or social disturbance, the miserable relics of these

peripatetic newsmen bawl the heads of the telegram or information in quiet London thoroughfares, to the disturbance of the residents. The race is very nearly extinct.
[Hotten] SEE *piper's news*

ruricolist An inhabitant of the country. [Johnson]

ruth Pity, compassion, from whence *ruthless*, pitiless, and *ruth-
ful*, compassionate. [Mackay]

rutterkin A crafty old knave. [Cotgrave]

sad bread Heavy bread, ill-made bread. Shakespeare calls it "distressful bread"—not the bread of distress, but the *panis gravis*, or ill-made bread eaten by the poor. [Brewer]

sailors' home A house built by subscription, for accomodation of seamen on moderate [incomes], and to rescue them from swindlers, crimps, &c. Sailors' homes are a great boon also to shipwrecked mariners. [Smyth] SEE *dower-house*

St. Patrick's needle In the phrase, *to have gone through St. Patrick's needle*, to have been in bankruptcy court. [Darlington]

sale-caller Within the present century, it was customary for the parish clerk to announce to the congregation in the churchyard, at the service, the sales to be held shortly, and also to offer rewards for the recovery of stolen goods or stray cattle, and other notices. [Dickinson]

sale-drink The gratuitous liquor handed round at a sale. [J. Wright] It is considered mean to go only for the drinking and neither to bid nor buy. [Dickinson]

saloop A greasy-looking beverage, formerly sold on stalls at early morning, prepared from a powder made of the root of the *Orchis mascula* . . . Charles Lamb, in one of his papers, has left some account of this drinkable which he says was, of

saloop

all preparations, the most grateful to the stomachs of young chimney-sweeps. The present generation has no knowledge of this drink, except that derived from books. The word "slops," as applied to weak, warm drink, is very likely derived from the Cockney pronunciation of *saloop*. [Hotten] SEE *ninny-broth, purl, scandal-broth*

salvatella A vein in the arm terminating in the fingers, formerly regarded as having peculiar influence on the health when opened; from Latin *salvus*, safe. [Stormonth] The ancients recommended this vein [also called the *vena amoris*] to be opened in certain diseases, as in melancholic and hypochondriacal affections, and they attribute to such abstraction of blood considerable efficacy in the cure of disease; hence its name. [Dunglison] SEE *wedding finger*

sandillions Numbers like the sand on the seashore. [Davies]

sand-knocker A man who grinds sandstone into grit, and sells it from door to door for sanding floors. [Taylor]

satyriasis An irresistible desire in man to have frequent connexion with females, accompanied with the power of doing so without exhaustion. The causes are commonly obscure. Sometimes the abuse of aphrodisiacs has occasioned it. The principal symptoms are: almost constant erection, irresistible and almost constant desire for venery, [and] frequent nocturnal pollutions. Cold lotions, the cold bath, a mild diet, active exercise, &c., are the only means that can be adopted for its removal. [Dunglison] As it occurs in females, it is the *nymphomania furibunda*. [Hoblyn]

say-shot An opportunity in a game to regain, by one stroke, all that one had previously lost. [Warrack]

scalch A morning drink. *Scotland* [J. Wright] Some excellent brandy was served round immediately, according to the custom of the Highlands, where a dram is generally taken every day. They call it a *scalch*. SEE *dew-drink, purl, saloop*

scalds The scalds were the poets and the musicians of the ancient northern nations. They resembled the bards of the Britons, and were held in equal veneration by their countrymen. The scalds were considered as necessary appendages to royalty, and even inferior chieftains had their poets to record their actions and indulge their vanity. [Strutt] SEE *rhyming-ware*

scandal-broth Tea. The reference is to the gossip held by some of the womenkind over their cups, which cheer but not inebriate. Also called *chatter-broth*. [Halliwell] SEE *spermologer*

scart To scratch; [whence] *scart-free*, without a scratch or the slightest injury. [Mackay] To *scart one's buttons*, to draw one's hand down the breast of another so as to touch the buttons with one's nails; a mode of challenging to battle among boys; perhaps a relique of some ancient mode of hostile defiance. [Jamieson]

scaum Insincere talk; banter. One listening to a letter being read will, at a characteristic passage, say of the writer, "That's like his *scaum*," like his trick of talk, being more humourous than sincere. The term is also applied to scornfully abusive language. [Robinson, GMY]

sclent-bean A fragrant bean carried in snuff-boxes to perfume the snuff. [Warrack]

scleroticks Medicines which harden and consolidate the parts they are applied to. [Quincy] SEE *colleticks*

scotale Scotale is an extortion prohibited by the statute of *Charta de Foresta*, and it is where any officer of the forest keepes an ale-house, to the intent that he may have the custome of the inhabitants within the forest to come and spend their money with him, and for that he shall winke at their offences committed within the forest. [Rastell] It is compounded of *scot* and *ale*, which by transposition of the words is otherwise called an *aleshot*, and by the Welshmen *cymmhorth*. [Blount, *LD*] SEE *tineman*

screever A man who draws with coloured chalks on the pavement figures of our Savior crowned with thorns, specimens of elaborate writing, thunderstorms, ships on fire, &c. The men who attend these pavement chalkings, and receive halfpence and sixpences from the admirers of street art, are not always the draughtsmen. The artist, or *screever*, draws, perhaps, in half-a-dozen places in the course of a morning, and rents the spots out to as many cadaverous-looking men who, when anyone looks hard at them, will commence to dabble clumsily with the short pieces of chalks they always keep at hand. There are imposters of this kind in higher walks of art. [Hotten]

scrug A person is said to *scrug his bonnet* when he snatches it by the pique, and lifts it up, or cocks it on his brow, that he may look smart, bold or fierce. Allied perhaps to the English verb, *to shrug*. [Jamieson]

scrutineer An inquirer; a searcher; an examiner. [Annandale]

scruttle To save money with difficulty; to scrape together. *Lancashire* [J. Wright]

scruze To squeeze; to compress. Perhaps [from] *screw*. This word, though now disused by writers, is still preserved, at least in its corruption, to *scrouge*, in London jargon. [Johnson]

scuggery A state of concealment, especially in the phrase, *in scuggery*. [Atkinson]

sculsh Any trashy sweetmeats or unripe fruit, such as schoolchildren are fond of eating. [Mackay] SEE *eattocks*

scumfished Smothered, suffocated. [Holloway]

scunt Bankrupt; used in marble games. When a boy has lost all his marbles, he is said to be *scunt*. The word appears to be a variant of *skinned*, which is used in the same sense. [Addy]

sea-dog A meteor seen on the horizon before sunset or after sunset, viewed by sailors as a sure portent of bad weather. [Warrack] SEE *furole*, *weatherwiser*

sea-lawyer An idle, litigious "long-shorer," more given to question orders than to obey them. One of the pests of the navy as well as the mercantile marine. Also, a name given to the tiger-shark. [Smyth] A captious or scheming fo'csle hand; whence *sea-lawyering*, argument with officers. [Farmer] SEE *quodlibetarian*

seasurrounded Encircled by the sea. [R. Coxe] SEE *demi-island*

second-scent An expression framed on the model of *second-sight* ["the power of seeing prophetic visions"], meaning a presage, by means of the sense of smell, that death is near at hand. [R. Hunter] SEE *carfumish, feff, natkin, odor of sanctity*

seeksorrow One who contrives to give himself vexation. [Johnson]

sensorium In anatomy, the seat of common sense, that part of the brain where the nerves from the organs of all the senses terminate . . . which is the beginning of the *medulla oblongata*. [Bailey]

sentence-silver Money paid by the person losing his case and by the prosecutor also, towards the salary of the judges. [Warrack]

serpentine-verse A verse which begins and ends with the same words, as "Greater grows the love of pelf, as pelf itself grows greater." [R. Hunter]

shachled-shoes A contemptuous term for a person of whom no further use can be made, especially for a woman discarded by her lover. [From] *shachle*, to twist or wear out of shape. *Scotland* [J. Wright] SEE *knotchel, widow-bewitched*

shail-about To move as if the bones were loose in their sockets, like a ripe nut in its shell. [From] Belgian *schale*, shell. *Norfolk* [Holloway] SEE *ruckle*

shamming-Abraham An odd phrase, common among soldiers and sailors, used when they counterfeit sickness or infirmity. It was probably derived from the *Abraham-men* of Shakespeare's time, described in *King Lear*. [Halliwell]

shammocking Shambling; a *shammocking man* means an idle, good-for-nothing person; a *shammocking dog* means almost a thievish, stealing dog. *New Forest* [Cope]

shanks'-pony On foot. [Taylor] SEE *ride-and-tie*

shazzying Dancing. [Wilkinson]

sheep-bed In the phrase, *to take a sheep-bed*, to sleep on the grass, like a sheep. [J. Wright] When a labourer had drunk too much, he would *take a sheep-bed*. [Dartnell] SEE *palliard*

sheep's-eye A modest, diffident, or sly look, such as lovers cast at their mistresses. [R. Coxe] *To cast a sheep's eye*, to look amorously or wantonly. [Nares]

shepherd's book A book published at irregular intervals extending over several years, and containing the distinctive marks, ear-mark and *smit* [marking with a soft, red stone] of the stocks of heaf-going sheep of the farms in the fell, or mountain districts of Cumberland, Westmoreland and northern Lancashire. With the ear-mark and smit together, the marks of upwards of six hundred farms or estates are given herein. . . . Each stock is illustrated by the diagram of a sheep, nearly one thousand in all. [Ellwood] SEE *clicking-fork't, rounstow*

shilling-dreadful A short novel, one of a sensational character, published in one volume and sold for a shilling. [R. Hunter] SEE *trencher-poetry*

shimshank To peep inquisitively; to pry; to sneak. *Cornwall* [J. Wright] SEE *hedge-creep*

shirty To make anybody *shirty*, or to *get anybody's shirt out*, is to

get him into a furious passion, or very angry, by teasing, jeering or bantering him, or by playing a practical joke upon
him. [Taylor] SEE *rudderish*

Shivelavat's-hen A hen which has ceased to lay; figuratively,
a woman past child-bearing. [Mactaggart]

shivviness The feeling of roughness caused by a new under-
garment. [Robinson, GWW]

shoot-finger This was a term in use with the Anglo-Saxons
from its necessity in archery, and it is now called the *trigger-
finger*, from its equal importance in modern fire-arms. The
mutilation of this member was always a most punishable offence, for which the laws of King Alfred inflicted a penalty
of fifteen shillings, which at that time probably was a sum
beyond the bowman's means. [Smyth]

shuttle-gathering An expedient for stopping weaving facto-
ries without breaking the machinery. The shuttles from the
looms were forcibly gathered and taken away by the discon-
tented weavers and, as they could not be replaced for several weeks, business had to be suspended. [Taylor]

sic-sic Said to pigs when called to the trough by those who
think little that they are speaking pure Saxon, in which *sic*
is a pig. [Watson]

side-slip An illegitimate child. [R. Hunter] SEE *queer-gotten,
special-bastard*

silly season The period when nobody is supposed to be in London, when there are no parliamentary debates to publish,
and when [newspaper] editors are at their wits'-ends to fill

silly season

their papers with readable matter. All kinds of crazes on political and social subjects are then ventilated: gigantic gooseberries, monstrous births, and strange showers then become plentiful, columns are devoted to matters which would not at any other time receive consideration and, so far as the newspapers are concerned, silliness is at a premium. [Hotten] SEE *piper's news*

sithcundman The oldest inhabitant; the one who knows what happened a long time since. The chief man in a town, district or parish. [Mackay]

six-water grog A sea-term for the weakest grog possible—six portions of water to one of rum—hardly enough spirit to swear by. [Hotten] Given as a punishment for neglect or drunkenness, instead of the usual *four-water*, which is one part rum, four parts water, lime-juice and sugar. [Smyth] SEE *drowning the miller, water-bewitched*

sizers Certain poor scholars at Cambridge, annually elected, who got their dinners—including *sizings*—from what was left at the upper, or Fellows' table, free, or nearly so. They paid rent of rooms, and some other fees, on a lower scale than the *pensioners,* or ordinary students, and were equal with the "battlers" and "servitors" at Oxford. [Hotten] SEE *alms-drink*

skenchback Having strong personal or family characteristics; remarkable in appearance; easily recognizable. *Yorkshire, Northamptonshire* [J. Wright] SEE *double-sib, slughorne*

skewboglish Said, but not very commonly, of a shying horse. *Lincolnshire* [Halliwell]

skilly Poor broth, served to prisoners in *hulks* [prison ships]. Oatmeal and water in which meat has been boiled. Hence, *skillygalee,* or *burgoo,* the drink made with oatmeal and sugar, and served to seamen in lieu of cocoa as late as 1814. [Smyth] SEE *whey-wullions*

skimmerton To *ride skimmerton* is an exhibition of riding by two persons in a cart, having skimmers and ladels, with which they carry on a sort of warfare or gambols, designed to ridicule someone who, unfortunately, possesses an unfaithful wife. [Jennings] SEE *stang, whores-hunting*

skybosh Practical joking, "larking," tomfoolery; generally in the phrase, *to give one skybosh,* to put a stop to larking. *Lancashire* [J. Wright] SEE *shirty*

slammack To walk slovenly, to do anything awkwardly; *slammocks, slammerkin, slamkin,* an awkward, waddling person, a sloven. The sound of dabbling in the wet, or of the flapping of loose clothes is represented by the syllables *slab* or *slap, slamp, slam.* . . . The meaning seems to vibrate between slackness or laziness of action, and the expression of neglect by the figure of loose, trailing, or flappy clothes. [Wedgwood]

slape ale Plain ale, as opposed to ale medicated with wormwood or scurvy-grass, or mixed with any other liquor. [Ray] SEE *purl*

slathertrash One whose shoes are down at the heel; a slovenly-dressed person; a slattern. [Darlington]

slawterpooch A slovenly, ungainly person. *Cornwall* [J. Wright]

sleepaway To die without disease, peaceably, and by gradual decrease of the powers of nature. [Mackay] SEE *enthasy, placeparted*

slench To hunt about privately with a view to stealing food. *Midlands* [J. Wright]

slister To idle away time; to be lazy and careless. [Robinson, *DOL*] SEE *causey-webs*

slocking-stone A rich stone of ore from a mine, exhibited in order to induce adventurers to proceed in a mining scheme. [Worcester]

slockster One that *slocks*, or entices away another man's servants. [Blount, G]

sloom To sleep heavily and soundly; distinguished from *slumber*, to sleep lightly. *Northern England* [Mackay]

slotter To make a noise with the palate while eating. To feed like an animal; [whence] *slotterhodge*, a coarse-feeding animal. [Allied with] *slote*, the pit of the stomach. [Mackay] SEE *roxle*

sloven's year A wonderfully prosperous season, when even a bad farmer has good crops. [Dartnell] SEE *stepmother-year*

slughorne A hereditary feature or characteristic of a family or race. [Warrack] SEE *double-sib, skenchback*

slut-grate Grating in the hearth through which the ashes fall, leaving the cinders. [T. Wright] It has the name from saving Cinderella the trouble of sifting the cinders. [Evans]

smell-feast A parasite, a habitual diner out; a sponge. [Mackay] A feast at which the guests are supposed to feed upon the odours of the viands. [R. Hunter] SEE *sorn*

smell-smock A lover of women; a great wencher. [Nares] SEE *carpet-knight, mulierosity*

smittlish Infectious; contagious. [Brockett] From the old Saxon *smittan* and Dutch *smetten*, to spot or infect; whence our word *smut*. [Ray]

smoking match Smoking matches are usually made for tobacco-boxes, or some other trifling prizes, and may be performed two ways: The first is a trial among the candidates who shall smoke a pipe full of tobacco in the shortest time; the second is precisely the reverse, for he who can keep the tobacco alight within his pipe, and retain it there the longest, receives the reward. [Strutt] SEE *grinning match*

smoothery Medicine or physical ointment to take away hair. [Blount, G]

smouster To eat clandestinely. *Fife* [Jamieson] SEE *chimble*, *motch*

smuce A contemptive epithet applied to any place. "Such a *smuce!*" a teetotaller would say in relating his experience of a gin-shop. [Robinson, *DOL*]

snapper-back In American football, the player, usually the center, who puts the ball in play. [Mathews]

snattock A scrap or fragment. [Nares]

sneerag A child's toy, made of the larger bone of a pig's foot and two worsted strings, and worked so as to give a snoring sound. [Warrack]

snirp To shrink, to shrivel up. [Addy]

snirtle To attempt to suppress one's laughter; [from] *snirt*, a short, suppressed laugh. [Mackay]

snogly gear'd Handsomely drest. [Ray]

snood The snood was a riband with which a Scotch lass braided her hair, and was the emblem of her maiden character. When she married she changed the snood for the *curch*, or *coif*. But if she lost the name of virgin before she obtained that of wife, she "lost her silken snood," and was not privileged to assume the curch. [Brewer]

snoutfair A person with a handsome countenance. [Nares] SEE *bellibone, cowfyne, pigsnye*

snow-blossom A snow-flake. [Cope]

snow-bones The patches of snow seen stretching along ridges, in ruts, or in furrows, after a thaw. [Warrack]

snow-broth Snow, when it is melted and trodden into slush. [Taylor]

snuff-dipping A mode of taking tobacco practised by some of the lower class of women in the United States, consisting of dipping a brush among snuff and rubbing the teeth and gums with it. [R. Hunter]

soft-wind Flattery. *Lanark* [J. Wright] SEE *court-holy-water, puzzomous*

somewhen At some time or other. [Long]

soom To drink a long draught with a sucking sound of the mouth, as if in great thirst or with great relish. [Mackay]

sooterkin A kind of false birth fabled to be produced by the Dutch women from sitting over their stoves. [Walker]

sorditude Filthinesse. [Cockeram]

sorn A word common in Scotland to express the art of fastening one's self upon another, to feast and lodge, unasked and unwelcome, almost equivalent to the word, to *sponge* in England. In Scotland, to go and sorn upon a man for a dinner would be in England to go "take pot-luck" with him, he not expecting you. . . . It is said to be a corruption of *sojourn*, to tarry from day to day, and to have been derived from the ancient practice in unsettled times of bands of armed men, living at free quarters upon the people when passing through a country. [Mackay] SEE *flattybouch*

sororiation A swelling, or becoming round and embossed, like a young virgin's breasts. [Phillips]

soul-case The body. [Halliwell]

sowl Anything eaten with bread. [Bailey] SEE *browis, fattycakes*

spanwhengle To shake or knock about violently. [Warrack]

sparrow's ticket Literally, no ticket at all. [To] *come in on a sparrow's ticket:* to climb a fence and gain free admission to a cricket or football ground. [Baker]

special-bastard A child born of parents before marriage, the parties afterwards intermarrying. [R. Hunter] SEE *double-sib, queer-gotten, side-slip*

spermologer A picker-up of trivia, of current news; a gossipmonger; what we today would call a *columnist.* [Shipley]

spidireen The name of an imaginary ship, sometimes mentioned by sailors. If a sailor be asked what ship he belongs to, and does not wish to tell, he will most probably reply, "The *spidireen* frigate, with nine decks and ne'er a bottom." [Hotten]

spinning-house An English house of correction so-called because women of loose character had to spin or beat hemp there as a punishment. [R. Hunter]

spiritual incest Sexual incest between two persons who have a spiritual alliance by means of baptism or confirmation. [Buck]

spittle sermons Sermons preached at the *spittle* [hospital] in a pulpit erected expressly for the purpose. [Brewer]

spleenful Angry; peevish; fretful; melancholy. [Johnson] SEE *cut-fingered, waspish*

spooning Spooning, in rowing, is dipping the oars so little in the water as merely to skim the surface. The resistance being very small, much water is thrown up and more disturbed. [Brewer]

spoops At Harvard College, a weak, silly fellow, or one who is disliked on account of his foolish actions is called a *spoops*, or *spoopsy*. [Hall]

spouse-breach In law, adultery. [Ogilvie] SEE *bedswerver, preternuptual*

sproag To run among the [hay]stacks after the girls at night. [Jamieson]

spuddle To go about a trifling business as if it were a matter of grave importance. To assume airs of importance without occasion. [Mackay]

squiggle To shake and wash a fluid about in the mouth, with the lips closed. [From] *quaggle*, quagmire, or from the sound produced by the act. *Norfolk* [Holloway] SEE *glox*

squinant Very medicinable, [as] camel's meat. [Blount, G]

squiny In Old English, to look asquint. [Stormonth] To look sidelong or invitingly, as a prostitute on the prowl. [Shipley]

stable-meal The liquor consumed in an inn by farmers by way

spuddle

of remunerating the innkeeper for accomodating their
horses during the day. [Jamieson]

stable-stand Stable-stand is when a man is found with a
crossebowe bent, ready to shoote at any deere, or with a
long bow, or else standing with greyhounds in his lease,
ready to let slip. [Manwood] Stable-stand is one of the four
evidences or presumptions whereby a man is convinced to
intend the stealing of a king's deer in the forest. [Cowell]
SEE *dog-draw, yburpananseca*

stale-drunk A man is said to be *stale-drunk* when he has been
drunk overnight, and has doctored himself with stimulants

a little too much in the morning—when he has tried too many of the "hairs of the dog that bit him." If this state of things is long continued, it is often called "same old drunk." [Hotten] SEE *crapulous*

stalking-horse If the fowl are so shy . . . that there be no way to come at them fairly, you must lead forth your *stalking-horse*, being some old jade, trained up for that purpose, that will not startle much at the report of a gun. . . . You may also make an artificial ox or cow, which you may use when your horse is discovered through much use. [Worlidge]

stampointed Bewildered, overcome with astonishment. A hunted rabbit in its fright is said to be *stumpointed. Norfolk, Suffolk* [J. Wright] SEE *struck-comickil*

stang To *ride the stang* is to be carried on a pole on men's shoulders through the town for the amusement of a hooting crowd. This is a derisive punishment for a breech of decorum or morality, especially on the part of a married man. [Taylor] SEE *skimmerton*

statute-cap Woollen cap ordered by an act of parliament of 1571 to be worn "upon the Saboth and Holy Daye," by "all and every person and persons above the age of syxe yeres," except women and certain officials. [Onions] The act was passed for the benefit of the cappers, or cap-makers, and the penalty for violating it was ten groats. [Phin]

stauging A custom prevalent in Cumberland on Christmas eve. The maid-servants of the substantial families, if found out of doors, are seized by the young men, placed in chairs and borne to the nearest beer-shop, where they are detained until they buy their liberty by small sums, which are usually expended by their captors in liquor. [Halliwell]

steel-wine Wine in which steel filings have been placed for some time. It is used medicinally. [R. Hunter] SEE *tincture of the moon*

stelliscript That which is written in the stars. He who desires to learn what good they prefigure must read them from west to east; but if he would be forwarned of evil, he must read from north to south. [Davies] SEE *extramundane, firmament, primovant*

stepmother-year A cold, unfavorable year. [Warrack] SEE *sloven's year*

stiff-quean A lusty wench. [Holloway] SEE *rigmutton*

stirrup-dram A glass of ardent spirits, or draught of ale, given by the landlord of an inn to his guest when about to depart. [Jamieson]

stirrup-verse A verse at parting. [Halliwell]

stockjobber A low wretch who gets money by buying and selling in the funds. [Johnson] SEE *landjobber*

stomachous Angry, disdainfull. [Phillips]

stoopgallant Something that humbles the great, that makes the *gallant* a mere man. Originally a name for the "sweating sickness," a fever of swift fatality in the fifteenth and sixteenth centuries. [Shipley]

stove-of-sickness A fit of illness accompanied by a high temperature. *Lanark* [J. Wright]

strange-achieved Gained in foreign lands; gained by wrong means. [Onions]

strigil An instrument to scrape off sweat from wrestlers; a horse-comb or scraper. [J. Coxe]

struck-comickil Rendered speechless or bewildered by surprise or terror. [Taylor] SEE *stampointed*

strumphusher Perhaps, an usher to strumpets. [Nares]

strut-speech A pompous, talkative, ignorant fellow. [Taylor]

stultiloquent Given to foolish talk or babbling. [R. Hunter]

stupration Adultery, rape; deflouring a virgin. [Blount, G] SEE *bedswerver, spouse-breach*

suaviloquy A sweet or pleasant manner of speaking. [Phillips]

succubus A devil or demon which assumes a woman's shape to lie with a man. [Bailey] Some authors have used this word synonymously with *nightmare*. Others mean by it a female phantom with which a man, in his sleep, sometimes believes he has intercourse, as *incubus*, applied to the male phantom with which a female may dream she is similarly situate. [Dunglison] SEE *incubus*

sullen-sick Sick with ill-humour. [Davies] *Sick of the sullens*, very gloomy or morose. [Halliwell]

sun-suckers The sun's rays as they sometimes appear in showery weather, popularly believed to suck up the water from the earth into the sun, there to be converted into rain, and held to be a sign of coming showers. [Jackson] SEE *devil's smiles, falling-weather*

surface-coal Cow-dung, widely used for fuel. *Texas* [Wentworth]

surfeitwater Water that cures *surfeits* . . . sickness or satiety caused by overfulness. [Johnson] SEE *crapulous*

swaff To come one over the other, like waves upon the shore. [Mackay]

swarble The motion of the limbs in ascending the boll of a tree in contradistinction of climbing amongst the branches. [Halliwell]

swazz To swagger. [Brogden]

swell-mobsman A member of the *swell-mob* . . . the class of pickpockets who go about genteelly dressed. [Annandale] SEE *Tyburn-blossom*

swigman A swygman goeth with a pedlers pack. [Awdeley] These Irish swig-men, being much alike . . . carry pins, points and laces, and such like wares about. [Head]

swine-greun A swine's snout; [from] *graun naufus, superius labrum* [an upper lip muscle]. Whence our English word *grin*, because in grinning the muscles of the upper lip are contracted. [Ray] SEE *bibitory, flepper*

swullocking Very sultry. The clouds are said to look *swallocky* in very hot weather, just previous to a thunderstorm. *Norfolk, Sussex* [Holloway] SEE *devil's smiles, Noah's ark*

tachygraphy The art of swift writing. [Bailey]

tadago-pie A pie made of abortive pigs from a sow that has miscarried. *Cornwall* [Halliwell]

taghairm A mode of divination formerly used by the Highlanders. A person was wrapped up in the skin of a newly slain bullock, and deposited beside a water-fall, or at the bottom of a precipice, or in some other strange, wild and unusual situation where the scenery around him suggested nothing but objects of horror. In this situation he revolved in his mind the question proposed, and whatever was impressed upon him by his exalted imagination passed for the inspiration of the disembodied spirits who haunt their desolate recesses. [Jamieson]

tagliacotian A nose of wax . . . An inhabitant of Bruxels had his nose cut off in a cumbate, and a new one of another man's flesh set in its stead by Taliacotius, a famous chirurgeon of Bononia. [Blount, G] *Taliacotian operation*, a surgical operation for forming an artificial nose. [Annandale]

tailor's mense When a tailor works at his customer's house, and has his meals there, he leaves a little food on his plate to show that he has had enough. This is called the *tailor's mense* ["respect"], and has come to be applied to all food left on the plate. [Brockett]

tailor's mense

talkingstock An object of notice or conversation. [Davies] SEE *gazingstock, pointing-stock*

tankard of October A tankard of the best and strongest ale, brewed in October. [Brewer] SEE *clank-knapper, peg-tankard, pitch-tankard*

tantrels Idle people that will not fix to any employment. [Ray] SEE *causey-webs*

tap the admiral To suck liquor from a cask by a straw, said to have been done with the rum-cask in which Lord Nelson's body was brought to England, to such an extent as to leave the gallant admiral [high and] dry. [Hotten] Opprobriously applied to those who would drink "anything." [Smyth] SEE *anti-guggler, ullage*

tarans The little spectres, or souls of unbaptised infants, [who] were often seen flitting among the woods and secret places, bewailing in soft voices their hard fate. [Pennant]

tarantismus Disease characterized by excessive avidity for dancing at the sound of instruments, and which was ascribed . . . to the bite of the tarantula. [Dunglison]

tavern fox To "hunt a tavern fox," to be drunk. [Davies]

tavern-token A token issued by a tavernkeeper and current only at his house. [Later] a tavern-token was simply an ordinary [coin] so called because most of them would travel to the tavern. To "swallow a tavern-token," a euphemism, to be drunk. [R. Hunter]

tazzled Entangled; [from] *tazz*, a rough, untidy head of hair. [T. Wright] SEE *elflocks*

teaty-wad A small portion of moist sugar tied up in a rag of linen of the shape and size of a woman's nipple, given to quiet an infant when the mother is unable to attend. [Halliwell]

teemful Pregnant, heavy, fruitful, brimful. [Webster]

tent-pegging A game or sport consisting in trying to prick a tent-peg out of the ground with a spear or lance while riding at full speed. [R. Hunter]

terebinthine Of or belonging to *turpentine*, or the tree out of which it issues ... A faire, clear and moist kind of rosin which issues out of the Larx and Turpentine tree. It is good to be put into ointments and emplaisters, for it glews, cleanses and heals wounds. It may be licked [mixed] in with honey, and then it cleanses the breast and gently looseth the belly, provoking urine and driving out the [kidney] stone and gravel. [Blount, G]

thenadays In those days; in time past. Opposed or correlative to *nowadays*. [Whitney]

thick-eyed Not *dim-eyed*, as some have it, but the absorbed look of a man in deep thought. [Phin] SEE *brownstudy*

thieves' vinegar

thieves' Latin Cant terms used by thieves. [Davies] SEE *cat-Latin, dog-Latin*

thieves' vinegar A kind of vinegar made by digesting rosemary tops, sage-leaves, etc., anciently believed to be an antidote against the plague. It derived its name and popularity from the story that four thieves who plundered the bodies of the dead during plague ascribed their impunity to this preparation. [R. Hunter]

thigger One who draws on others for subsistence in a genteel sort of way. [Jamieson]

thinnify To make thin. [Davies]

thirding A custom practised at the universities, where two-thirds of the original price is allowed by the upholsterers to the students for household goods returned to them within one year. [Halliwell]

thirty-pound knights James I became the subject of much ridicule, not quite unmerited, for putting honours to sale. He created the *Order of the Baronet*, which he disposed of for a sum of money; and it seems that he sold common knighthood as low as £30. [Nares]

thorough cough Coughing and breaking wind backwards at the same time. [Grose, *DVT*]

thrunched Very angry, displeased. [Mackay]

thumbassing Fumbling with the hands as if the fingers were all thumbs. [Holland] SEE *cow-handed*

thumb-buttercake A piece of oat-cake or bread upon which butter has been spread with the thumb-nail. [Taylor] SEE *sowl*

thumbit A piece of meat eaten on bread, so called from the thumb being placed on it. [Long]

thumb-licking, smit-thumbs An ancient mode of confirming a bargain. In a bargain between two Highlanders, each of them wets the ball of his thumb with his mouth and then joining them together; it is esteemed a very binding act. [Jamieson]

thumbstal A *thimble*. A cap of leather put on a sore thumb to preserve it from air or accident. [Jones]

thunderstone A stone fabulously supposed to be emitted by thunder. [Sheridan] It is not impossible, however, that the opinions of the ancients in regard to thunderstones have been derived from the fact that in some cases, that passage of electric current through the soil produces vitrified tubes known as *fulgerites*. These tubes have often been dug out and might readily be taken for thunder-bolts, or *thunderstones*. [Phin]

thurindale A pewter flagon holding about three pints. [T. Wright] SEE *pottle-draught, woolsorter*

thwankin Used of clouds, mingling in thick and gloomy succession. [Warrack] SEE *devil's smiles, Noah's ark*

timber-taster A person who examines timber. [T. Wright]

tincture of the moon In chymistry, a dissolution of some of the more rarified parts of silver, made into wine. [Bailey] SEE *steel-wine*

tineman An officer of the forest who took care of vert [vegetation] or venison in the night. [Bailey] These are they that

now are called *foresters* or *keepers*. [Manwood] SEE *batilbaby*,
scotale

tinker's toast The [burnt] crust at the side of a loaf which has
been one of the outside loaves of a batch. [Patterson] SEE
bread-rasp, *geo-graffy*, *kissingcrust*

tinny-hunters Persons whose practice it is to attend fires for
the purpose of plundering the unfortunate sufferers; probably from the Gaelic *teine*, fire. [Farmer]

tit-faggots Small faggots. [T. Wright]

tittynope A small quantity of anything left over. *Yorkshire* [J.
Wright]

toad-bag A small piece of linen having a limb from a living
toad sewn up inside, to be worn round the sufferer's neck
and next to the skin, the twitching movements of which
limb gave, so it was said, "a turn" to the blood of the wearer,
and effected a radical change in his constitution, [used] by a
conjurer or "white wizard." [R. Hunter]

toad-eater Originally a mountebank's man, whose duty was to
swallow, or pretend to swallow any kind of garbage; a fawn-
ing sycophant. Said to be a version of *avaler des couleuvres*,
to swallow adders, to put up with all sorts of indignities
without resentment. [Donald] SEE *lion's-provider*

tongue-fence Debate, discussion, argument. *Milton* [Whitney]

tongue-shot Reach of the tongue; *out of tongue-shot*, out of ear-
shot. [Davies] SEE *eyeshot*

tongue-whaled Severely scolded; [from] Saxon *walan*, to wale.
[Holloway] SEE *curtain-lecture*, *xantippe*

tooth-music [The sound of] chewing. [Grose, *DVT*] SEE *chimble*

tooth-soape Of the heads of mice being burned is made that excellent powder, for scouring and cleansing of the teeth called *tooth-soape,* unto which if spikenard [lavender] be added or mingled, it will take away any filthy scent or stronge savour in the mouth. [Topsell]

tootle To try the notes in an under tone, as a singing-bird, before beginning the whole song. [T. Wright]

tosher One who, on the Thames, steals copper from ships' bottoms. [Smyth]

tourkin-lamb A tourkin-lamb is one taken from its dam, and given to another ewe that has lost her own by death. In this case, the shepherd takes the skin of the dead lamb and puts it on the back of the one that is to suck the ewe which has lost her lamb, and thus deceives her so that she allows the stranger to suck. *Scotland* [J. Wright] SEE *minnie, tulchan*

tout-hill, toot-hill A hill or eminence on which, in time of danger or war, a man was stationed to *tout* or blow a horn as a signal; [whence] the modern *touter,* a man who stands at the door of a shop, to entice people in. [Mackay] Of frequent occurrence in place-names. The *Tuthill-stairs* in Newcastle ascend the eminence called *Tout-hill* in Bourne's map, 1736. . . . In old formal gardens, a tout-hill was an artificial mound formed for the purpose of commanding a prospect. [Heslop]

town-bull A bull belonging to a parish; figuratively a noisy, rude fellow. [Sheridan] One that rides all the women he meets. [B.E.]

town-husband An officer of a parish who collects the moneys from the parents of illegitimate children for the maintenance of the latter. *Eastern England* [Halliwell] SEE *queer-gotten*

town-of-trees A grove near a dwelling-place. [Jago]

town-rout To go gossiping about from house to house. [Evans]

towrus Among hunters, a roebuck eager for copulation is said to *go to his towrus*. [Bailey] SEE *breem, clicketing, eassin*

trageleph An animal resembling the goat and the elephant. [J. Coxe] The great and blackish deere called a *stone-buck,*

transcribbler

deer-goat, or *goat-hart* because conceived between a buck, goat and hind. [Blount, G]

transcribbler One who transcribes hastily or carelessly; hence a mere copier. [Whitney]

transfeminate To change from a male to a female. [R. Hunter] To turn from woman to man, or from one sex to another. [Blount, G] SEE *ambosexans, unsex*

traumaticks Herbs or drugs good for the cure of wounds. [Bailey]

traveltainted Fatigued with travel. [Johnson]

treating-house Restaurant. [Davies]

trencher-poetry Rhymes to be traded for bread; verses written so as to secure a patron. [Shipley] SEE *rhyming-ware, scalds*

trilemma Any choice between three alternatives. [R. Hunter]

trinkle To eavesdrop. [T. Wright]

trophy-money A duty of four pounds paid annually by house-keepers for the drums, colour, &c. for their respective companies of militia; [from] *trophy*, a monument set up in a place where enemies were vanquished, with their ensigns, warlike harness and other spoils hanging on it. [Bailey]

trouble-mirth One who mars or disturbs enjoyment or mirth, as a person of morose disposition; a spoil-sport. [R. Hunter]

tuft-hunter A hanger-on to persons of quality or wealth; one who seeks the society of wealthy people. Originally university slang, but now general. [Hotten] From the *tuft* or tassel in the cap worn by noblemen at the English universities. [Lyons]

tulchan A calf-skin stuffed in the rude similitude of a calf, similar enough to deceive the imperfect perceptive organs of a cow. At milking times the tulchan, with head duly bent, was set as if to suck; the fond cow, looking round, fancied that her calf was busy and that all was right, and so gave her milk freely, which the cunning maid was straining in white abundance into the pail all the while. . . . King James's Scotch bishops were, by the Scotch people, derisively called *tulchan bishops*. [Carlyle] SEE *tourkin-lamb*

tulipomania A reckless mania for the purchase of tulip-bulbs in the seventeenth century. Beckman says it rose to its greatest height in the years 1634–37. A root of the species called *Viceroy* sold for £250, [and] *Semper Augustus* more than double that sum. The tulips were grown in Holland, but the mania which spread over Europe was a mere stock-jobbing speculation. [Brewer]

tunnage Money paid by the ton. [Webster]

turnpike man A parson, because the clergy collect their tolls at our entrance into and exit from the world. [Grose, *DVT*]

tutting A tea-drinking for women, succeeded by stronger potations in the company of the other sex, and ending, as might be expected, in scenes of ribaldry and debauchery. It is so-called, I believe, in Lincoln; in other places in the country it is known by the name of a *bun-feast*. The custom is now obsolete, or nearly so, to the amelioration, it is hoped, of society. [Halliwell]

twee To "be in a twee," to be overcome with fear or vexation. [T. Wright]

tutting

tweeny-maid A servant who assisted both cook and house-maid. [J. Wright]

two pun' ten An expression used by assistants to each other, in shops, when a customer of suspected honesty makes his appearance. The phrase refers to "two eyes upon ten fingers," shortened as a money term to *two pun' ten*. When a supposed thief is present, one shopman asks the other if that two pun' (*pound*) ten matter was ever settled. The [second shopman] knows at once what is meant, and keeps a careful watch upon the person being served. If it is not convenient to speak, a piece of paper is handed to the same assistant, bearing the, to him, very significant amount of £2.10. [Hotten]

twychild A man or woman in extreme old age or second child-hood; from *twy*, twice. *Shakespeare* [Mackay]

Tyburn-blossom A young thief or pickpocket, who in time will ripen into fruit born by the "deadly nevergreen," the great gallows known as *Tyburn Tree*. [Grose, *DVT*] SEE *figging-law, little snakesman, moon curser, swell-mobsman*

tyromancy Divining by the coagulation of cheese. [Gaule]

ugsumness Terribleness. [Coles]

ullage Of a cask, what such a vessel wants of being full. [Phillips] *Oiler, ouiller* [means] to fill to the brim, to swill with drink. In the South of France, when the flask is nearly full they add a little oil to prevent evaporation, so that *to oil the flask* is equivalent to filling it to the brim. In Provence, *oliar* signifies to annoint with oil, and also to fill up a cask. [From] French *eullage*, to fill up to the bung-hole. [Wedgwood]

umstroke The edge of a circle. [From] Anglo-Saxon *ym, ymb, um*, around, round about. [R. Hunter] SEE *chilihedron*

unbeer Impatient. [Ray]

unbosom To reveal in confidence. [Webster]

undercold A cold caught from the ground. A term associated with loose apparel. [Robinson, GMY]

underhung A person whose lower jaw projects is said to be *under-hung*. [Davies]

underskinker An under-drawer; a tapster's helper. [Phin]

unky Lonesome. In Gloucester, *unked* is lonely. Seems to be a corruption of *uncouth*. [Pegge]

unlarded Not *interlarded*. [R. Hunter] SEE *interlard*

unlicked Unpolished, as an "unlicked cub" is a raw, unpolished youth. This word is probably borrowed from the saying that a bear's cub is a shapeless mass until the mother has *licked it into shape*. [Holloway]

unnun To depose, dismiss or release from the condition or vows of a nun. [R. Hunter]

unpregnant Not prolific; not quick of wit. *Shakespeare* [Browne] Unapt for business. [Skeat]

unsex To make otherwise than the sex commonly is. [Walker] To deprive of sex, or the qualities of the sex to which one belongs; usually to deprive of the qualities of a woman; to *unwoman*. [R. Hunter] SEE *transfeminate*

unshingling A practice of taking a hat from a traveller's head in the darkness of night during his wanderings through the streets. [Baker] SEE *ruffler*

unsnod Rough, not smooth; in disorder; from *snod*, preterit of *snid*, mown, shorn, pruned. *Snodgrass*, a well-known name, means mown or shorn grass. [Mackay]

unsoulclogged Not weighed down in spirit. [Davies]

unspoken water Water from under a bridge over which the living pass and the dead are carried, brought in the dawn or twilight to the house of a sick person, without the bearer's speaking either in going or returning. [Warrack] The modes of application are various. Sometimes the invalid takes three draughts of it before anything is spoken; sometimes it is thrown over the house, the vessel in which it was contained being thrown after it. The superstitious believe this to be one of the most powerful charms that can be employed for restoring a sick person to health. [Jamieson]

upknocking, knocking up One of the curious ways of earning a livelihood in the manufacturing towns. The "knocker up" wakes the different hands of a mill who cannot wake themselves, so that they can get to their work in time, and not be fined for being too late. The general pay of the knocker up is twopence a head, per week. I remember once a witness, being asked what he was, answering, "A *knocker up*," deeming it, evidently, as much a trade as a tailor or a baker. [Leigh] SEE *knocking-up-stick*

upputting Lodging, entertainment for man and beast. *Scotland, Northumberland* [R. Hunter]

upscores To *be upscores* with a person, to be even with him. *Yorkshire* [J. Wright]

urf A stunted, ill-grown child; nearly synonymous with *urk*; whence the diminutive, *urchin*. [Mackay] SEE *urled*

urinal pulse A critical pulse, fancied to denote an approaching evacuation of urine. [Dunglison]

urled *To be urled;* it is spoken of such as do not grow. Hence, an *urling,* a little dwarfish person. In the South they call such *knurles.* [Ray] SEE *urf*

urtication The act of whipping a palsied or benumbed limb with nettles to restore its feeling; from *urtica,* a nettle. [Hoblyn] A sort of flagellation with nettles, used with the intention of exciting the skin. [Dunglison]

uterine brother A brother by the mother's side. [Bouvier]

V has two powers expressed in modern English by two characters, *V* consonant and *U* vowel, which ought to be considered as two letters. But, as they were long confounded while
the two uses were annexed to one form, the old custom still
continues to be followed. [Johnson]

vagation A wandering. [Coles] SEE *mundivagant*

vagitus The distressing cry of persons under surgical operations.
[Hooper]

vaniloquence Much talke. [Cockeram]

varnishing-day A day before the opening of a picture exhibition, on which exhibitors have the privilege of retouching
or varnishing their pictures, after they have placed them on
the walls. [Whitney]

varnishing-day

velocipede A light vehicle or conveyance consisting mainly of wheels, and driven or impelled by the feet of the rider or pair of riders. [Annandale] The mania for using these velocipedes commenced in France, spread to England, and afterwards to the United States, and occupied the attention of those addicted to athletic sports. . . . But their mode of locomotion proving of no practical value, the employment of velocipedes grew less, until now but few are used. [Zell]

verjuice An acid liquor prepared from very sour grapes or crabapples [along with "oil of unripe olive" and crab broth]. It is principally used in culinary preparations, although occasionally an ingredient in medicinal compounds. [Dunglison] From French *verd*, green, and *jus*, juice. [Zell] SEE *thieves' vinegar*

verter-water Water found in the hollows of tombstones and rocks, a charm for warts. [Warrack]

vigerage The loan shark's twenty percent weekly interest. "Five dollars for six" is the usual weekly arrangement. Small loans are most frequent, although very large sums are sometimes borrowed by influential citizens who wish to keep their transactions secret. [Goldin]

viridate To make green and lusty. [Blount, G]

virilia A man's privy members, the cutting off of which was felony by the common law, whether the party consented or not. [Blount, LD]

vocating Going about from place to place in an idle manner. From Latin, *voco*; the verb to *vocate*, to go about from place to place in an idle manner, is also occasionally used. [Jennings] SEE *causey-webs, sorn*

vomitory A door of a large building by which the crowd is let out; [from] Latin *vomitorius*. [Lyons]

vootery Deceit. [Lowsley]

vorago A gulf, a whirlpool, a quagmire, or marvellous deep place that sucks or swallows up even rivers, and whereout nothing can come. Also a gluttonous waste-gut and spend-all. [Blount, G] SEE *naufrage*

waesucks Alas! O, the pity. Scottish interjection. [R. Hunter]
SEE *yoicks*, *zuggers*

wager of battel In the old English law, a barbarous mode of trying facts among a rude people, founded on the supposition that heaven would always interpose and give the victory to the champions of truth and innocence. This mode of trial was abolished as late as A.D. 1818. [Bouvier]

walapang In Lombardic law, to disguise one's self in order to commit theft. [Tayler]

walking-supper A supper at which one dish was sent round the table, at which every person carved for himself. [T. Wright]

wallabee-track Colonial slang for the tramp. When a man in

Australia is "on the road," looking for employment, he is said to be "on the *wallabee-track*." [Hotten]

walleteer One who carries a wallet, a bag for carrying the necessities for a journey or march. [Ogilvie] SEE *gaberlunzie*

wallopy Loose-limbed. [Patterson]

wangary Soft and flabby. This is the regular word used by butchers to express the condition of meat which will not get solid, a very common fault in warm weather, or if the animal was out of condition when slaughtered. [Elworthy] SEE *cagmag*

warming-stone The bakers in our country take a certain pebble, which they call the warming-stone, which they put in the vaulture of their oven, for when that is white, the oven is hott. [Aubrey] A foot-warmer . . . first heated in the fire or on a stove, and afterward placed under the feet. It is chiefly made use of in driving in very cold weather. Soapstone is selected for this purpose because it stands the heat better than any other stone, not cracking or crumbling when exposed to sudden changes of temperature. [Whitney]

waspish Peevish; malignant; irritable. [Johnson] SEE *cutfingered*

water-bewitched Very weak tea, the third brew—or the first at some houses. Sometimes very weak tea is called *husband's tea*, in allusion to the wife taking the first brew, and leaving the rest for her husband. Also, grog much diluted. [Hotten] Bad tea, *geo-graffy*, five-water grog, and the like greatly di-

water-caster

luted drinks. [Smyth] Weak tea, punch coffee, &c. of which
the flavour is almost imperceptible from the super-
abundance of water in the mixture. *Norfolk, Sussex* [Hol-
loway] SEE *Adam's ale, dog's soup, drowning the miller,
six-water grog*

water-caster A mediciner who professes to tell the disease by
the cast or appearance of the urine, into a bottle of which
he puts certain ingredients or chemicals. While the changes
are going on, they are supposed to influence, sympatheti-
cally, the patient's complaint. [Robinson, *GWW*]

water-wolf In drinking out of a stream, a man is said to *swallow* *a water-wolf* which, it is said, lives and grows in his stomach. [Addy]

waveson Such goods as, after shipwreck, do appear swimming on the waves. [Cowell]

wayzgoose An entertainment given by a master printer to his workmen, marking the beginning of work by candle-light, usually about Bartholomew-tide. [Shipley] The derivation of this term is not generally known. It is from the old English word *wayz*, stubble. A stubble goose is a known dainty in our days. A wayz-goose was the head dish at the annual feast of the forefathers of our fraternity. [Timperley]

weaponsalve A salve which was supposed to cure the wound, being applied to the weapon that made it. [Johnson] The direction, "Bind the wound and grease the nail," is still common when a wound has been given with a rusty nail. Sir Kenelm Digby says the salve is sympathetic, and quotes several instances to prove that "as the sword is treated, the wound inflicted by it feels. Thus, if the instrument is kept wet, the wound will feel cool, if held to the fire, it will feel hot." [Brewer]

weatherspy A stargazer, astrologer, wizard. [Webster] SEE *planet-ruler, stelliscript*

weatherwiser Anything that foreshadows the weather. [R. Coxe] SEE *sea-dog*

wedbreaker An adulterer. [Wycliffe] SEE *bedswerver, preternuptual*

wedding finger Macrobius says the thumb is too busy to be set apart, the forefinger and little finger are only half protected, the middle finger is called *medicus*, and is too opprobrious for the purpose of honour, so only the little finger left is the *pronubus*, or wedding finger. [Brewer] The finger on which the ring is to be worn . . . by the opinion of the learned in ripping up and anatomising men's bodies, there is a vein of blood, called the *vena amoris*, which passeth from that finger to the heart. [Swinburne] SEE *mercurial-finger, salvatella*

weeping-ripe Ready to weep; ripe for weeping. [Nares]

weep-Irish To scream; to yell. [Halliwell]

wee-wow Wrong; in an unsettled state. [T. Wright] Apparently a reduplicated variant of *wow*, [from] Anglo-Saxon *woh*, crooked. [Whitney]

welwilly Benevolent. [Mackay]

wet finger To do a thing *with a wet finger* implies to do it with great ease. . . . It seems not very improbable that it alluded to the very inelegant custom of wetting the finger to turn over a book with more ease. . . . Those who practised this had little thought of the appearance of their books. [Nares] It probably means as easy as . . . rubbing out writing on a slate with a wet finger, or tracing a lady's name on the table with spilt wine. [Skeat] The illusion is to the old custom of spinning, in which the spinner constantly wetted the forefinger with the mouth. [Brewer]

whelm To overturn, upset; to push over. *Northern England* [J. Wright]

whetstone A liar's property. The term *whetstone*, for a liar, or for the prize for lying, seems to be very old and, according to Nares, was a standing jest among our ancient ancestors as a satirical premium to him who told the greatest lie. Ray puts, "He deserves a whetstone," among proverbial phrases denoting liars. [Elworthy]

whey-wullions Dish for dinner, formerly common among peasants, consisting of the porridge left at breakfast, beaten down with fresh whey, with an addition of oatmeal. [Warrack] SEE *skilly*

whiffinger A vagabond. [Warrack] SEE *gyrovagues, palliard*

whiffler The term is undoubtedly borrowed from *whiffle*, another name for a fife or small flute, for whifflers were originally those who preceded armies or processions as fifers or pipers. . . . In the process of time, the term *whiffler* . . . came to signify any person who went before in a procession. [Douce]

whipping-cheer [A] "banquet of lashes" with the whip. [Onions] A flogging, chastisement. [Phin] SEE *land-damn, mastigophorer*

white bonnet A name given to the person who, in a sale by auction, bids for his own goods, or who is employed by the owner for this purpose. This metaphoric term seems to signify a marked person, or one who deserves to be marked; in allusion, perhaps, to the custom in Italy by which the Jews are obliged to wear yellow bonnets for distinction, or of bankrupts wearing green bonnets, according to the laws of France. [Jamieson] SEE *bairman*

white-burying A burial during falling snow. [J. Wright] SEE *falling-weather*

white eye Military slang for a very strong and deleterious kind of whisky, so called because its potency is believed to turn the eyes round in their sockets, leaving the whites only visible. [Hotten] SEE *potsheen-twang*

white powder A noiseless gunpowder popularly supposed to be used by poachers. [Moor] Some conspirators in Queen Elizabeth's time confessed that they had intended to murder the queen with fire-arms charged with *white-powder*. But it is

white eye

not pretended that any such preparation was found in their possession. [Nares]

white serjeant A man fetched from the tavern or ale-house by his wife is said to be *arrested by the white serjeant*. [Grose, *DVT*]

whitesmith A worker in tinned iron. A finisher or polisher of iron-work, as distinguished from a [*blacksmith* or] *forge-man*. [Zell]

whores-hunting When a wife left her husband to live with another man, the villagers would assemble outside the guilty couple's house with a horse's head stuck on a pole, and would pull the jaw down by means of a sting tied through the animal's lower lip. [Hayden] SEE *stang*

whypjacke A whypjacke is one that by colour of a counterfaite lisence doth use to beg lyke a maryner. But hys chiefest trade is to rob b[o]oths in a faire, or to pilfer ware[s] from staules, which they call *heaving of the booth*. [Awdeley] SEE *mastigophorer, post-knight*

wicker A method of castrating a ram by enclosing his testicle within a slit stick. *Gloucestershire*. [Grose, *PG*] SEE *chaser*

widow-bewitched A woman who is separated from her husband. [Halliwell] SEE *shachled-shoes*

widow's piano Inferior instruments sold as bargains, so called from the ordinary advertisement announcing that a widow lady is compelled to sell her piano, for which she will take half price. [Brewer] SEE *music-duffer*

wikes *Wikes of the mouth*, corners of the mouth. [Ray]

wink-a-peeps The eyes. [Holland] SEE *Billy-winks*

winter-hedge A frame of wood on which linen is dried in the laundry after having been washed in winter, or when the weather will not allow of exposing it on the hedges out of doors. [Watson]

winter-love Cold or conventional love-making. [Davies]

winter's sisterhood A sisterhood devoted to perpetual chastity; hence, cold, barren. [Phin]

witch-mark A mark found on the body of every witch. There were three kinds or varieties of the witch-mark, the *horn-mark*, which was very hard, the *brief-mark*, which was very small, and the *feeling-mark*, in which there was a sense of pain. *Scotland* [J. Wright]

witch-pricker A witch-finder who discovered witches by pricking them [with] a wooden bodkin or pin . . . for the *witch-mark*. [Warrack]

witch's-stirrups Matted locks in a horse's mane. [Jackson] SEE *elflocks*

withy-cragged Said of a person whose neck is loose and pliant. [Halliwell]

witworm One who feeds on or likes wit. [Webster]

woken'd When the breath is stopt with over-hasty drinking. [Watson]

wolfshead An outlaw, meaning a person who might be killed with impugnity like a wolf. [Tayler]

woman-tired Henpecked. [R. Hunter] SEE *chicken-pecked*

womb-pipe The vulve, or privie passage. [Cotgrave]

wonder-wench A sweetheart. *Yorkshire* [J. Wright] SEE *belli-bone, cowfyne*

wood-body A person of a very violent temper. [Warrack]

woolsorter For many years, this term was used for half-a-pint of beer in a pint tankard. [Wilkinson] SEE *pottle-draught*

woolward To go *woolward*, in wool only without linen, a dress often enjoined as a penance by the Church of Rome. [Skeat] In an old book entitled *Customs of London*, the privilege called a *karyne* is said to be gained by certain observances of a penitential nature, the first of which was "to go wulward seven yeer." The word is one of the usual compounds of *ward*, meaning "toward the wool." [Nares]

woonkers Interjection expressive of wonderment or surprise. [Robinson, GMY] SEE *lorgeous-days*

wooze Marshy ground. [Davies]

wordify To put into words. *Yorkshire, Devonshire* [J. Wright]

word-pecker One that plays with words. [B.E.]

wrine A deep line in the face; a furrow; hence, the diminutive *wrinkle*, a small wrine. [Mackay]

wry-rumped Deformed in the lower part of the back. *Norfolk* [Holloway]

wuther An onomatopoeous word to signify the rustling of the wind among the branches. [Davies]

wuzzle To mingle. [Whitney]

X is a letter which, though found in Saxon words, begins no words in the English language. [Johnson] XX, as applied to ale and porter, signifies of the second quality, or doubly strong; XXX, of the third quality, or triply strong. A single X signifies of the first quality, or of the ordinary strength. [Ogilvie]

xanthodont Having yellow teeth, as a rodent. [Whitney]

xantippe A mouthing, scolding woman. [Smith] The wife of Socrates, the famous philosopher. Her alleged shrewish temper is proverbial, and her name has become the synonym for a scold. As an illustration of her shrewishness and the mild temper of her husband, we are told that on one occasion, after she had scolded him unmercifully until her tongue gave out, and yet without drawing forth the slightest remonstrance or exciting the least anger on his part, she emptied a vessel of dirty water over him. His only remark was that "after thunder we must naturally expect rain." [Phin] SEE *clapperclaw, curtain-lecture, tongue-whaled*

xyster A surgeon's instrument to scrape and shave bones with. [Browne]

yaffle To talk indistinctly, mincing the breath, as in the case of toothless persons. [Robinson, GMY]

yburpananseca The stealing of a calf or ram, or as much as a man can carry on his back. Skene could not tell the origin of the word, but Spelman says, "'Tis compounded of the letter *y*, for *you,* and *byryin,* which signifies a burthen, and *seca,* a sack, *i.e.* a burthen in a sack." [Blount, *LD*] SEE *dog-draw, bloody-hand*

yeepsen As much of anything as can be taken up in both hands together; a double handful. [Grose, PG] SEE *fingerfull, pugil*

yesterfang That which was taken, captured or caught on the previous day or former occasion. [Whitney]

yeth-hounds Hounds without heads, supposed to be animated by the spirits of children who have died without baptism.

yird-swine

These hounds are believed [according to] superstition current in Devonshire, to ramble among the woods at night making wailing noises. [Mackay]

yird-swine A mysterious, dreaded sort of animal, called the yird swine, was believed to live in graveyards, burrowing among the dead bodies and devouring them. [Gregor]

yoicks An old hunting cry; from the sound made. [R. Hunter] SEE *waesucks, zuggers*

yule-hole The last hole to which a man could stretch his belt at a Christmas feast. [Warrack]

zamzodden [From] *zam*, to heat for some time over the fire, but not to boil. [Holloway] Anything heated for a long time in a low heat so as to be in part spoiled . . . It is not improbable that this word is a compound of *semi*, Latin [for] half, and *seethe*, to boil, so that zamzodden will then mean, literally, *half-boiled*. [Jennings]

zeoman A settled or staid man, such I mean as being married and of some years, betaketh himself to stay in the place of his abode for the better maintenance of himself and his family, whereof the single sort have no regard, but are likely to be still fleeting, now hither now thither, which argueth want of stability in determination and resolution of judgement, for the execution of things of any importance. [Holinshed]

ziff A beard. [Baker]

zoldering An opprobrious epithet reserved for very wrathful occasions, but without more meaning than the force of sound conveys. [Robinson, GMY]

zonam solvere To deflower a virgin. Young maids, when they were married, were wont to have a marriage girdle tied about their middle, which their husband the first night of their marriage did untie. From [Latin] *zonam*, a soldier's or wedding belt, and *solvere*, to undo. [Blount, G]

zowerswopped Ill-natured. [T. Wright] The word implies a nature that is so thoroughly crabbed that the very *sap* is *soured*; [also] spelt *zower-zapped* and *zowerzop'd*. [Elworthy]

zuggers An interjection. This is a word, like others of the same class, the precise meaning of which is not easy to define. [Jennings] SEE *lorgeous-days, waesucks, yoicks*

zwodder A drowsy and stupid state of body or mind. Derived, most probably, from *sudor*, Latin [for] sweat. [Jennings]

zythepsary A brewhouse. [Coles]

BIBLIOGRAPHY

Addy, Sidney. *A Glossary of the Words Used in the Neighborhood of Sheffield*. London, 1888.

Andry, Nicholas. *Orthopaedia: The Art of Correcting and Preventing Deformities in Children*. London, 1743.

Annandale, Charles. *A Concise Dictionary of the English Language*. London, 1897.

Atkinson, John. *A Glossary of the Cleveland Dialect*. London, 1868.

Aubrey, John. *The Natural History of Wiltshire*. London, c. 1697 (1847).

Awdeley, John. *The Fraternitye of Vacabondes*. London, 1561.

Bailey, Nathaniel. *An Universal Etymological English Dictionary*. London, 1749.

Baker, Sidney J. *A Dictionary of Australian Slang*. Melbourne, 1943.

Barclay, James. *A Complete and Universal Dictionary of the English Language*. London, 1848.

Barrère, Albert, and C. Leland. *A Dictionary of Slang, Jargon and Cant*. London, 1889.

Batchelor, Thomas. *An Analysis of the English Language*. London, 1809.

B.E., Gent. *A New Dictionary of the Terms . . . of the Canting Crew*. London, c. 1690.

Bewick, Thomas. *The General History of Quadrapeds*. London, 1790.

Blancard, Stephen. *The Physical Dictionary*. London, 1708.

Blount, Thomas. *Glossographia*. London, 1656, 1661.

————. *A Law Dictionary and Glossary*. London, 1670 (1717).

Borlase, William. *Antiquities of the County of Cornwall*. Oxford, 1758.

Bouvier, John. *A Law Dictionary Adapted to the . . . United States*. Philadelphia, 1839.

Brand, John. *Observations on Popular Antiquities*. London, 1777–1841.

Brande, William T. *A Dictionary of Science, Literature and Art*. London, 1842.

Brewer, E. Cobham. *Dictionary of Phrase and Fable*. Philadelphia, 1887, 1898.

Brockett, John. *A Glossary of North Country Words*. Newcastle upon Tyne, 1825.

Brogden, J. Ellett. *Provincial Words and Expressions Current in Lincolnshire*. London, 1866.

Brown, John. *Dictionary of the Holy Bible*. 1806.

Browne, Thomas. *The Union Dictionary*. London, 1810.

Buck, Charles. *A Theological Dictionary*. Philadelphia, 1835.

Budworth, Joseph. *A Fortnight's Ramble to the Lakes of Westmoreland*. London, 1792.

Bullokar, John. *An English Expositor*. London, 1616.

Burne, Charlotte. *Shropshire Folk-Lore: A Sheaf of Gleanings*. London, 1883.

Carew, Richard. *The Survey of Cornwall*. London, 1602.

Carlyle, Thomas. *Letters and Speeches of Cromwell*. London, 1845.

Carr, William. *The Dialect of Craven*. London, 1828.

Chambers, Ephraim. *Cyclopedia: An Universal Dictionary of Arts and Sciences*. London, 1728, 1751.

Chambers, Robert. *The Book of Days: A Miscellany of Popular Antiquities*. London, 1864.

Clapin, Sylva. *A New Dictionary of Americanisms*. New York, 1902.

Clarke, James. *A Survey of the Lakes of Cumberland*. London, 1787.

Cocker, Edward. *An English Dictionary*. London, 1704.

Cockeram, Henry. *The English Dictionary: An Interpreter of Hard English Words*. London, 1623.

Coles, Elisha. *An English Dictionary*. London, 1713.

Cope, William. *A Glossary of Hampshire Words and Phrases*. London, 1883.

Cotgrave, Randle. *A Dictionarie of the French and English Tongues*. London, 1611.

Cowell, John. *The Interpreter: The Signification of Words*. London, 1607 (1701).

Coxe, John. *A Medical Dictionary*. London, 1817.

Coxe, Richard. *A Pronouncing Dictionary*. London, 1813.

Crabb, George. *A Dictionary of General Knowledge*. New York, 1830.

Darlington, Thomas. *The Folk-Speech of South Cheshire*. London, 1887.

Dartnell, G. E., and E. H. Goddard. *A Glossary of Words Used in the County of Wiltshire*. London, 1893.

Davies, T. Lewis. *A Supplemental English Glossary*. London, 1881.

De Vere, Schele. *Americanisms: The English of the New World*. New York, 1871.

Dickinson, William. *A Glossary of the Words and Phrases [of] Cumberland*. London, 1878, 1899.

Donald, James. *Chambers's Etymological Dictionary of the English Language*. London, 1877.

Douce, Francis. *Illustrations of Shakespeare and of Ancient Manners*. London, 1807.

Dunglison, Robley. *A Dictionary of Medical Science*. Philadelphia, 1844.

Dyce, Alexander. *A Glossary to the Works of William Shakespeare*. London, 1902.

Dyche, Thomas, and William Pardon. *A New General English Dictionary*. London, 1740.

Dyer, T. F. Thiselton. *Folk-Lore of Shakespeare*. New York, 1884.

Easther, Alfred. *A Glossary of the Dialect of Almondbury and Huddlesfield*. London, 1883.

Edmondston, Thomas. *A Glossary of the Shetland and Orkney Dialect*. Edinburgh, 1866.

Ellwood, Thomas. *Lakeland and Iceland: A Glossary of English Dialect Words*. London, 1895.

Elworthy, Frederic. *A Vocabulary or Glossary [of Exmoor]*. London, 1778 (1879).

Elyot, Thomas. *Dictionary*. London, 1545.

Evans, Arthur B. *Leicestershire Words, Phrases and Proverbs*. London, 1881.

Falconer, William. *A Universal Dictionary of the Marine*. London, 1769.

Farmer, J. S., and W. E. Henley. *Slang and Its Analogs*. New York, 1904.

Fenning, Daniel. *The Royal English Dictionary*. London, 1775.

Florio, John. *Queen Anna's New World of Words*. London, 1611.

Forby, Robert. *The Vocabulary of East Anglia*. London, 1830.

Gaule, John. *The Mag-Astro-Mancer, or The Magicall Astrologicall-Diviner Posed*. London, 1651.

Goldin, Hyman E. *The Dictionary of American Underworld Lingo*. New York, 1950.

Grant, William. *The Scottish National Dictionary*. Edinburgh, 1931–41.

Gregor, Walter. *Folklore of North-East Scotland*. London, 1881.

Grose, Francis. *A Classical Dictionary of the Vulgar Tongue*. London, 1796.

———. *A Provincial Glossary* and *Supplement*. London, 1811, 1814.

Hall, Benjamin. *A Collection of College Words and Customs*. Cambridge, 1856.

Halliwell, James. *A Dictionary of Archaic and Provincial Words*. London, 1855.

Hampson, R. T. *Dates and Customs of the Middle Ages*. London, 1841.

Harland, John, and T. Wilkinson. *Lancashire Folk-Lore*. London, 1867.

Hayden, Eleanor. *Travels Round a Berkshire Village*. London, 1901.

Hazlitt, W. C. *Faiths and Folklore of the British Isles*. London, 1905.

Head, Richard. *The Canting Academy, or The Devil's Cabinet Opened*. London, 1673.

Heslop, R. O. *A Glossary of Northumberland Words*. London, 1892.

Hoblyn, Richard. *A Dictionary of Terms Used in Medicine*. Philadelphia, 1859.

Holinshed, Raphael. *The Chronicles of England, Scotland and Ireland*. London, 1577.

Holland, Robert. *A Glossary of the Words Used in the County of Chester*. London, 1884–86.

Holloway, William. *A General Dictionary of Provincialisms*. Lewes, Sussex, 1838.

Hollyband, Claudius. *A Dictionary of French and English*. London, 1593.

Hone, William. *The Every-Day Book*. London, 1826.

Hooper, Robert. *Lexicon Medicum: A Compendious Medical Dictionary*. London, 1798–1839.

Hotten, John Camden. *The Slang Dictionary*. London, 1887.

Howard, John. *The State of Prisons in England and Wales*. London, 1777.

Hull, Eleanor. *Folklore of the British Isles*. London, 1928.

Hunter, Joseph. *The Hallamshire Glossary*. London, 1829.

Hunter, Robert. *The Encyclopaedic Dictionary*. Philadelphia, 1894.

Huntley, Richard. *A Glossary of the Cotswold Dialect*. London, 1868.

Irwin, Godfrey. *American Tramp and Underworld Slang*. New York, 1931.

Jackson, Georgina. *Shropshire Word-Book*. London, 1879–81.

Jago, Fred. *The Ancient Language and the Dialect of Cornwall*. Truro, 1882.

Jamieson, John. *An Etymological Dictionary of the Scottish Language and Supplement*. Paisley, 1879, 1887.

Jennings, James. *The Dialect of the West of England*. London, 1869.

Johnson, Samuel. *A Dictionary of the English Language*. London, 1755.

Jones, Stephen. *A General Pronouncing and Explanatory Dictionary*. London, 1818.

Jonson, Ben. *The Alchemist*. London, 1610.

Judges, A. V. *The Elizabethan Underworld*. New York, 1930.

Kennett, White. "Manuscript Collection of Provincial Words." c. 1700.

Kersey, John. *Dictionarium Anglo-Britannicum, or A General English Dictionary*. London, 1721–72.

Kirkby, B. *Lakeland Words*. London, 1898.

Leigh, Edgerton. *A Glossary of Words Used in the Dialect of Cheshire*. London, 1877.

Long, W. H. *A Dictionary of the Isle of Wight Dialect*. London, 1886.

Lowsley, Major. *A Glossary of Berkshire Words and Phrases*. London, 1888.

Lyons, Daniel. *The American Dictionary of the English Language*. London, 1897.

Mackay, Charles. *Lost Beauties of the English Language*. New York, 1874.

Mactaggart, John. *The Scottish Gallovidian Encyclopedia*. London, 1824.

Manwood, John. *A Brief Collection of the Lawes of the Forest*. London, 1598.

Marshall, William. *The Rural Economy of Yorkshire*. London, 1788.

Mathews, Mitford. *A Dictionary of Americanisms on Historical Principles*. Chicago, 1956.

Mayhew, Henry. *London Labour and the London Poor*. London, 1861.

Moor, Edward. *Suffolk Words and Phrases*. London, 1823.

Morris, Edward. *A Dictionary of Austral English*. London, 1898.

Nares, Robert. *A Glossary [of . . .] the Works of English Authors*. London, 1859.

Nicholson, D. *Manuscript Collection of Caithness Words*.

Nodal, John, and George Milner. *A Glossary of the Lancashire Dialect*. London, 1875.

Northall, G. F. *Folk-Phrases of Four Counties*. London, 1894.

Ogilvie, John. *The Comprehensive English Dictionary*. London, 1865.

Onions, C. T. *A Shakespeare Glossary*. Oxford, 1911.

Palsgrave, Jehan. *Dictionary of the French Language*. Paris, 1530 (1852).

Parish, W. D. *Dictionary of the Sussex Dialect*. Lewes, 1875.

Patterson, W. Hugh. *A Glossary of Words of Antrim and Down*. London, 1880.

Peacock, Edward. *A Glossary of Words Used in Lincolnshire*. London, 1877.

Pegge, Samuel. *An Alphabet of Kenticisms*. London, 1735–36.

Pennant, Thomas. *A Tour in Scotland*. London, 1769.

Pennecuik, Alexander. *A Description of the Shire of Tweedale*. London, 1715.

Peter, T. C. "Manuscript Collection of Cornish Words."

Phillips, Edward. *The New World of English Words*. London, 1658–1706.

Phin, John. *The Shakespeare Cyclopaedia and New Glossary*. New York, 1902.

Quincy, John. *Lexicon Physico-Medicum: A New Medical Dictionary*. London, 1719.

Rankin, Alexander. *The History of France*. London, 1801.

Rastell, William. *The Exposicions of the Termes of the Lawes of England*. London, 1624, 1641.

Ray, John. *A Collection of Words . . . Proper to the Northern [and] Southern Counties*. London, 1691.

Robinson, C. Clough. *A Dialect of Leeds*. London, 1862.

———. *A Glossary of Mid-Yorkshire*. London, 1876.

Robinson, Francis K. *A Glossary of Words Used in the Neighborhood of Whitby*. London, 1876.

———. *A Glossary of Yorkshire Words and Phrases*. London, 1855.

Scott, William. *A Dictionary of the English Language*. London, 1791.

Sheridan, Thomas. *A Complete Dictionary of the English Language*. London, 1790.

Shipley, Joseph. *Dictionary of Early English*. New York, 1955.

Sinclair, John. *The Statistical Account of Scotland*. Edinburgh, 1791.

Skeat, Walter. *A Glossary of Tudor and Stuart Words*. Oxford, 1914.

Smith, Alexander. *The Thieves' New Canting Dictionary*. London, 1719.

Smyth, William. *The Sailor's Word-Book: An Alphabetical Digest*. London, 1867.

Stanyhurst, Richard. *The Historie of Ireland*. London, 1577.

Sternberg, Thomas. *The Dialect and Folk-Lore of Northamptonshire*. London, 1851.

Stormonth, James. *A Dictionary of the English Language*. Edinburgh, 1884.

Stow, John. *Survay of London*. London, 1598.

Stroud, I. *The Judicial Dictionary of Words and Phrases*. London, 1890.

Strutt, Joseph. *The Sports and Pastimes of the People of England*. London, 1876.

Swinburne, Henry. *A Treatise of Spousals, or Matrimonial Contracts*. London, 1686.

Tayler, Thomas. *A Law Glossary*. New York, 1856.

Taylor, Francis. *The Folk-Speech of South Lancashire*. Manchester, 1901.

Thoresby, Ralph. *A Glossary of Yorkshire Words*. London, 1718.

Timperley, C. H. *A Dictionary of Printers and Printing*. London, 1839.

Topsell, Edward. *The Historie of Four-Footed Beastes*. London, 1607.

Tyrwhitt, Thomas. Glossary, *The Poetical Works of Chaucer*. London, 1871.

Walker, John. *A Critical Pronouncing Dictionary and Expositor of the English Language*. Edinburgh, 1835.

Warrack, Alexander. *A Scots Dialectic Dictionary*. Edinburgh, 1911.

Watson, John. *Uncommon Words Used in Halifax*. London, 1775.

Webster, Noah. *A Compendious Dictionary of the English Language*. New Haven, 1806.

Wedgwood, Hensleigh. *A Dictionary of English Etymology*. New York, 1878.

Wentworth, Harold. *American Dialect Dictionary*. New York, 1944.

Whitney, William. *The Century Cyclopedia and Dictionary*. New York, 1889.

Wilkinson, John. *A Leeds Dialect Glossary and Lore*. London, 1924.

Worcester, Joseph. *A Dictionary of the English Language*. Boston, 1881.

Worlidge, John. *Systema Agriculturae*. London, 1675.

Wright, Joseph. *The English Dialect Dictionary*. Oxford, 1896–1905.

Wright, Thomas. *Dictionary of Obsolete and Provincial English*. London, 1857.

Zell, T. Ellwood. *Popular Encyclopedia: A Universal Dictionary*. Philadelphia, 1871.